GARDENING
IN
MINIATURE

GARDENING
IN
MINIATURE

Small Plants for Gardens, Window Boxes and Containers

MARTIN BAXENDALE

WARD LOCK

Text © Martin Baxendale 1990, 1992
Line drawings © Ward Lock Ltd 1990, 1992

First published in Great Britain in 1990
by Ward Lock Limited, Villiers House,
41/47 Strand, London WC2N 5JE, a Cassell
Company.

First published as paperback 1992

House editor Denis Ingram
Designed by Anita Ruddell
Text filmset in 11/12 Garamond Light
by Columns of Reading Ltd
Printed and bound in Hong Kong
by Wing King Tong Co. Ltd.

British Library Cataloguing in Publication Data
Baxendale, Martin
Gardening in miniature,
1. Miniature gardens
I. Title
635.967

ISBN 0 7063 7080 5

CONTENTS

PREFACE

Miniature plants have always fascinated gardeners and are invaluable both as space-saving planting choices where growing room is strictly limited and for creating appealing miniature-garden features and effects.

The following chapters aim to provide the gardener with a comprehensive guide to the various types of small and miniature hardy ornamental plants, shrubs, trees and bulbs, the situations in which they may be used, and the special garden features which may be conjured up with them.

Owners of small gardens should find these chapters especially useful, as an aid to selecting neat-growing plants and constructing mini-garden features to suit their very restricted spaces. But these enchanting plants and features will, of course, enhance any garden from the smallest to the very largest.

M. B.

One of the many attractions of miniature plants is that a wide range may be grown in a small space.

THE MAGIC OF GARDENING IN MINIATURE

Miniature plants, bulbs, shrubs and trees possess a special magical appeal that has captivated generation after generation of keen gardeners. Few seem able to resist the spell cast by these little gems while many, like myself, become so thoroughly hooked that the love of miniature plants grows into a lifelong passion.

I fell under the spell as a schoolboy on a holiday trip with my mother and father (both knowledgeable gardeners) to a famous Cotswold alpine plant nursery now, sadly, closed down.

The first thing to catch my eye as we walked into the nursery yard was a marvellous collection of old stone sinks and troughs lovingly and artistically planted with an enchanting array of tiny trees, shrubs and plants, each one a delightful little garden in miniature.

It was love at first sight as I wandered amongst them, stroking the tightly-packed foliage of perfectly spire-shaped dwarf junipers that were (as I learned later) over 30 years old yet less than 60 cm (2 ft) in height, bending to admire the brilliant sky-blue stars of dainty spring gentians, and discovering at every turn the flower-studded cushions and rosettes of countless more miniature delights.

Totally bewitched by the sheer charm and elegance of those little plants and trees, I came away enthralled with the prospect of creating such wonderful miniature gardens of my own. We left laden with plants, and within a few weeks I had built and planted my first rock garden and started what was, over the years, to become a series of mini-gardens in containers.

▫ The appeal of miniature plants ▫

I am sure that for most gardeners it is this magical notion of making miniature gardens complete with tiny trees, shrubs and plants that appeals most and which first attracts them to small plants like alpines and dwarf conifers. That was certainly the case with me.

But if you get hooked then you soon come to love miniature plants for themselves as much as for the joy of creating little gardens and landscapes with them. Who could fail to fall for the delicate and refined beauty of a dainty alpine wildflower, the elegance of a miniature daffodil or little species crocus (so much more enchanting than their larger-flowered hybrid cousins), or the perfect shapeliness in miniature of the tiniest dwarf conifers?

And, being miniatures, they are eminently 'collectable', since you can build up quite an extensive collection even in a restricted growing area. This, of course, also makes miniature plants, bulbs, shrubs and trees ideal choices for small gardens, where they allow the gardener to squeeze a lot of variety into a little space. Equally, in a small garden miniature plants are far less likely to outgrow their allotted space and become a nuisance than larger border plants, shrubs and trees.

Not that miniature plants are only useful where space is limited. Naturally, they have many uses in gardens of all sizes, and the special features that can be created with them will enhance any garden from the smallest to the largest.

□ Features and uses □

■ *Rock gardens and raised beds*
The rock garden is the most traditional feature that may be created with miniature plants and is usually the first idea that springs to the gardener's mind. With its slopes and valleys, it offers the most realistic setting in which to attempt the miniature mountain landscape effects that alpine enthusiasts strive for. Yet it is far from the only special garden feature that can be contrived with small plants. And it is certainly not the only place in the garden where miniature plants look and feel at home.

All miniature plants, bulbs, shrubs and trees are as happy in raised beds as on rock gardens, and a raised bed planted as a miniature garden or mini-landscape makes an equally fascinating attraction.

Even the most demanding and fussy alpine plants will thrive just as well in the free-draining soil conditions of a raised bed as they would on a rock garden, and rocks may be incorporated for effect in a raised bed, if you wish, just as in a more traditional rock garden. While they are, of course, not essential (alpines will thrive with or without them) rocks do complete the picture beautifully.

■ *Beds and borders*
Many miniature plants, bulbs, shrubs and trees are also quite at home in ordinary garden beds and borders, where they are extremely useful as low-growing frontal or edging plants, and where they provide a variety and contrast of height and scale alongside larger border plants and shrubs. Indeed, in very small gardens where growing space is severely limited the more usual range of larger plants and shrubs may even be completely replaced in beds and borders with a selection of less space-hungry miniature plants and shrubs; quite literally creating an entire garden in miniature.

The conifer and heather bed is a popular, attractive and easy-to-maintain garden feature. Choose dwarf conifers and heathers for a wide range of heights, shapes and foliage tints, select heather varieties to flower in different seasons, perhaps even add a few rocks if you wish, and you'll have a miniature landscape garden that will provide colour and evergreen interest throughout the year. It makes an excellent combination.

Peat beds make it possible for those of us who garden on limy soil to grow some of those sumptuous lime-hating plants, like rhododendrons and azaleas, which would otherwise fail in our ordinary beds and borders.

Unfortunately peat is not particularly cheap and you do need quite a lot even for a small bed, so here it really makes sense to go for the gardening in miniature approach. And a truly stunning lime-haters' mini-garden may easily be conjured up with the likes of dwarf rhododendrons, miniature azaleas and a range of beautiful lime-hating small plants such as the gorgeous blue-flowered autumn gentians.

■ *Containers, greenhouses and frames*

Of course planting containers, such as troughs, sinks, tubs and even large pots are ideal homes for the kinds of wonderful miniature gardens which captivated me and held me spellbound in that nursery yard many years ago. Even in a small container it is surprising what can be achieved with a dwarf conifer or shrub and a handful of miniature plants and bulbs. Indeed, these truly miniature self-contained gardens are surely the most alluring and enchanting of all, and I have yet to meet the gardener who did not long to try his or her own hand at this fascinating form of gardening after once seeing a skilfully-planted mini-garden in a lovely old stone sink or trough.

Small and miniature plants and bulbs are, naturally, excellent choices for window boxes. And even here it is quite possible to create permanent mini-gardens with dwarf conifers or shrubs, miniature perennial plants and dwarf bulbs (instead of the more usual seasonal bedding plants) to give colour and interest all year round.

Under glass, too, miniature plants are a delight. Given the protection of an unheated greenhouse, conservatory or coldframe, many of these small plants offer an even lovelier display than in the open garden, their dainty flowers unsullied by rain and soil-splashes, lasting that much longer when protected from the ravages of the weather. Miniature gardens may be composed here as well, either in large pots or in permanent beds. Alternatively, small plants, bulbs and shrubs in pots kept in a coldframe or outdoor plunge bed may be brought into the greenhouse as their different flowering seasons come around, to provide a constant but ever-changing display.

Whatever plan is devised, it is certainly a comfortable delight for the gardener to be able to enjoy a collection of miniature plants under cover of a greenhouse or conservatory when the weather outside is inclement. And, of course, a large range of miniature plants may be accommodated even in a small greenhouse or conservatory, giving the gardener (as always when gardening in miniature) excellent value for growing space.

■ *Paving, alpine lawns and pools*

In paving, small plants are useful for adding colour and interest to paths, patios and other paved areas, planted in cracks and gaps between the slabs. They may also be planted in gravelled paths, drives and suchlike areas to the same purpose. In these situations, as well as adding colour and interest, low-growing plants help to soften the harsh, hard look of large expanses of paving or gravel. And it is quite possible, in this way, to actually turn a paved or gravelled area or path into a mini-garden, making a real feature out of what would otherwise be simply a bare utilitarian space.

A truly charming effect may also be contrived by naturalizing dwarf bulbs in a patch of grass to produce a miniature 'alpine lawn' effect, the tiny bulb flowers spearing through the turf in spring (and in autumn, too, if you select bulbs for both seasons) just as they do in natural alpine meadows. A corner of a lawn given over to such a feature is a real delight, well worth the small trouble of having to mow carefully and leave the grass a little longer until the bulb leaves die down. This is a particularly good scheme for areas of grass beneath trees where turf tends to grow patchy anyway, making a colourful feature out of what might otherwise be something of an eyesore in the garden.

Miniature garden pools stocked with small aquatic plants are as fascinating and magical as miniature gardens and just as easy to create. Particularly suited to small gardens, they make an exquisite feature in any garden, large or small. But more about these and other miniature gardening features in later chapters.

□ Making plans □

The same basic rules of good gardening apply when planning and planting a miniature garden as when designing and planting on a larger scale. If you want to ensure the best possible results, bear these elementary guidelines in mind from the earliest stages.

Firstly, take as much care over planning as you would if you were designing a full-size garden. It may seem a little silly to actually draw up plans for such a small planting area, but this really is just as good an idea as it would be if you were tackling a larger area of beds, borders and lawns.

Actually putting your plans down on paper is always the best way to make a start. It helps you to spot mistakes and make improvements at an early stage, avoiding problems and disappointments later on. Play around on paper with different layouts and planting combinations, trying out various ideas before settling on your final scheme. Remember that what you want from a mini-garden is exactly the same as you would wish from a full-size garden: colour and interest in all seasons of the year, plenty of variety in the height, shape and foliage of the plants, and a pleasing, balanced overall design.

■ *A balanced plant mix*

Of course you will usually want the main flowering display from a miniature garden (just as in a larger garden) to come in spring and summer. But always aim to plan for some colour and interest in the other seasons as well, to ensure that your mini-garden offers something worth seeing all year round. So, when choosing plants for spring and summer colour do not forget to balance them with at least one or two plants or bulbs to flower in autumn and winter. And remember that evergreen plants, shrubs and conifers with colourful or handsome foliage will provide interest throughout the year and are therefore particularly valuable.

Aim also for a good mix of different plant heights and plenty of variety in plant types (i.e. plants with an upright growth habit, bushy plants, low-spreading and trailing plants) to ensure lots of contrast and diversity in your planting scheme. With small and miniature plants, where size differences are not always very great between one plant type and another, it can prove all too easy to overlook this vital point. But a planting plan which lacks this kind of well thought out diversity will generally end up looking boringly flat, lacking in interest and disappointing.

These kinds of carefully arranged foliage contrasts are especially valuable in any planting scheme because they make the plant groupings interesting and attractive to look at even when the plants are not flowering. And the contrasts need not necessarily be extreme to be effective. Widely differing combinations of leaf colours (green, grey, silver, gold etc.) will obviously produce the greatest visual impact and prove most eye-catching. But when grouping your plants together it is equally worthwhile considering, at all times, the possibilities of other more subtle foliage combinations as well. Even amongst green-leaved plants you will find all shades and types of green from light to dark, matt or glossy, which can offset one another very handsomely if thoughtfully combined with an eye to producing contrasts between neighbouring plants.

Size and shape of leaf are also important in creating good planting combinations. For example, small-leaved plants and large-leaved plants will offset one another well, each emphasizing the other's leaf character. Similarly, rounded leaves, deeply divided ferny leaves, long sword-shaped leaves etc. will contrast attractively with one another.

■ *Layout and contrasts*

The most basic planting layout rule for ordinary garden beds and borders is to group the tallest plants and shrubs at the back of the border or in the centre of a free-standing bed, grading down to smaller and smaller plants and shrubs as you move out towards the edge of the border or the bed.

This applies equally, as a basic principle, to miniature garden layouts. But do bear in mind that it is only a very general rule which needs to be broken from time to time in the interests of good layout design. The occasional smaller plant or shrub dotted amongst a group of tall plants and shrubs will, of course, introduce a note of contrast and add interest to the scheme. So, too, will a tall plant, shrub or conifer sprouting up from amongst a group of lower-growing plants.

Further contrast and interest may be contrived by deliberately placing together plants, shrubs or conifers with very different types of foliage or different foliage colours. This, again, is a basic device to make ordinary garden borders more eye-catching, and it can be used to equally good effect in miniature gardens.

So, wherever possible, try to avoid clumping too many similar-looking types of plant together in one spot. Rather, aim for a good mix of plant types with plenty of contrast not only in height and growth habit but also in foliage tints and leaf shapes.

When planning a largish miniature garden, such as a rock garden, remember also to spread around and evenly mix your plants for flowers in different seasons, so that you get a constant and evenly-spread display over the months. Avoid, for instance, inadvertently crowding most of your spring-flowering plants into one part of the mini-garden and most of the summer-flowering plants into another part. This will result in dull spots when one season's plants have finished their display.

All of this planning and design advice may seem rather ambitious and over-elaborate for the sort of small areas involved with miniature gardens. But it really is the basis of good general garden planting and applies as much to tiny growing areas as to larger ones.

With the very smallest of miniature gardens, such as sink and trough gardens, there will obviously be strict limits to what you can do in the way of layout and planting design. But even in those kinds of highly restricted situations it is worth bearing in mind at least some of these basic guidelines and applying them where you can. And where you have a little more space to play with, you may be surprised to find just how much scope there actually is for putting these principles into practice in a mini-garden.

■ *Plant growth rates and spacing*

On a more practical note, take care at the planning stage to check with reference books and nursery catalogues on the growth rates, ultimate size and cultural requirements of individual plants.

Speed of growth and eventual size are particularly vital factors in a miniature garden, where space is precious and small plants may quickly be smothered by over-vigorous neighbours. Not all alpines, dwarf conifers, dwarf shrubs and miniature bulbs are dainty little treasures, and some can prove a real menace, quickly outgrowing their allotted growing room and even completely taking over a small mini-garden.

So, the smaller the miniature garden, the more carefully you should select your plants, rigorously excluding any (no matter how tempting) which look like they might simply prove far too large or vigorous for the situation. And in the tiniest of mini-gardens, only the very neatest and daintiest should even be considered if you are to avoid overcrowding problems later on.

Be sure to space plants far enough apart to allow room for future growth. Young miniature plants, such as alpines and dwarf conifers, can look extremely tiny and lonely when first planted, spaced out across an expanse of all-too-bare soil, and the temptation to pack them in closer together for more immediate effect can be great. But that will only turn out to be a mistake in the long-run. Miniature plants need room to develop just as much as larger border plants and shrubs, and they will fill those spaces eventually – probably a lot faster than you would have imagined.

Try also, at the planning stage, to avoid siting very small and slow-growing plants next to vigorous fast-spreading plants. Otherwise you will only end up having to move plants or constantly having to chop back wandering shoots to prevent them strangling a neighbouring plant.

□ Cultivation requirements □

Checking up on the cultivation needs of your miniature plants before you begin planting is, naturally, just as important as for large border plants and shrubs; indeed more so, since many have rather more exacting cultural requirements than their larger cousins.

That does not mean that all miniature plants are particularly difficult to grow; far from it, in fact. Alpine plants, for example, do have a reputation for being a little tricky to please. Yet most really are quite easy once their basic needs are understood and catered for, while some will thrive quite happily under ordinary garden border conditions.

■ *Soil drainage*

As a general rule, what most miniature plants, trees, shrubs and bulbs either prefer or need in order to do well is free-draining soil, i.e. soil from which excess water drains away quickly after heavy rain. In slow-draining soil which remains waterlogged and sticky for long periods following rain, most miniature plants will tend to struggle or may even fail completely.

The reason for this is that most of the miniature plants that we grow in our gardens (or at least the wild plants from which they were raised) originate from mountainous regions where the soil is very stony and fast-draining, or from areas such as the Mediterranean where the summers are long and hot with little rain. No wonder, then, that these small plants, naturally adapted to extremely well-drained or even dry conditions, tend not to cope well with poorly-drained, wet garden soils.

If your soil is at all heavy and clayey, then thorough soil improvement before planting is essential. Working lashings of grit or coarse sand (or a mixture of both) into the planting site will improve the drainage. Adding humus at the same time, in the form of peat, garden compost, leafmould etc., will further help to lighten the soil and make it more suitable for miniature plants.

Even a reasonably good loamy garden soil, which is not particularly clayey, will still benefit from the addition of some of these drainage-improving materials if you plan to grow a range of miniature plants.

A miniature garden which is to be given over entirely or largely to alpine plants will, of course, need particular attention to drainage improvement, with

A superb collection of old stone sinks and troughs planted as miniature gardens with alpines, dwarf shrubs and conifers.

the addition of stone chippings (as well as some grit or coarse sand plus humus material) to imitate the soil conditions of their high-altitude homelands (see Chapter 2 for further advice).

Light sandy soils and gravelly soils are naturally free-draining and well suited to a wide range of miniature plants. All that is needed here is to add some humus material, to help retain summer moisture in these very dry soils and ensure that the roots of the tiny plants do not become desiccated during hot weather.

In containers, too, free-draining root conditions should be ensured for miniature plants, shrubs and bulbs. Always make sure that the planting container has adequate drainage holes in the base, and mix plenty of chippings or grit into the potting compost (see Chapter 8).

■ *Sun, shade and limy soil*

Apart from preferring or needing good drainage, miniature plants are just the same as larger plants and shrubs in having varying preferences regarding sun or shade, limy soil or non-limy soil, etc., and these should always be checked before planting. Like most garden plants in general, the majority of small and miniature plants do best in a sunny site and do not mind too much whether the soil is limy or not. However, some do enjoy shade and some will not grow in limy ground, so it is essential to make sure that the plants you choose are suited to the situation and the soil type.

Of course, this applies as much to miniature plants in containers as to plants in garden soil. When planning a miniature container garden, such as a trough, sink or window box garden, bear in mind where it is to be sited and select plants accordingly, choosing shade-loving plants for a shady site but avoiding these, and going for sun-lovers instead, where the container is intended for a sunnier situation. And if in your container garden you plan to grow lime-haters, such as dwarf rhododendrons or azaleas, then remember that they must have a lime-free potting compost (generally sold by garden centres and shops as 'ericaceous' compost).

□ Plant sources □

There is a vast range of small and miniature plants, shrubs, trees and bulbs available to today's gardeners, and a reasonable selection can usually be found by shopping around local garden centres and nurseries. But the choice that such local sources are able to offer is, naturally, limited.

For a much wider choice, you must turn to the catalogues of specialist growers. It really is well worthwhile taking the trouble to send for specialist catalogues or (better still, if you can manage it) to visit the nurseries and see the full range of available plants at first hand. Seeking out less commonplace and rarer plants is half the fun of gardening, and that is what will make your miniature gardens so much more interesting and exciting (both for yourself and your garden visitors) than if you simply settle for what you can find in local garden centre.

Rock gardening societies and their local groups are a great source for advice on many aspects of miniature gardening and for addresses of good miniature plant nurseries. They can usually suggest sources not only for alpine plants but also for small border plants, dwarf shrubs, conifers and other trees, and miniature bulbs.

CHAPTER TWO

BUILDING AND PLANTING ROCK GARDENS AND RAISED BEDS

As I mentioned in the previous chapter, the rock garden is by far the most traditional form of miniature gardening and is still the most popular feature that may be created using small and miniature plants. However, the raised bed has really come into vogue in recent years and makes an equally suitable home for rock plants, dwarf conifers, small shrubs and miniature bulbs.

Incidentally, the raised bed also offers the gardener the opportunity to create attractive wall gardens by planting in holes purposely built into the side of the bed. Similar wall garden features may, of course, be made of any retaining wall with suitable planting holes. But more on this subject later.

What both the rock garden and the raised bed provide, if properly constructed, are the well-drained soil conditions that alpines and many other small plants must have if they are to grow well. This is achieved by a combination of raising the soil above the surrounding ground level and adding drainage-improving materials.

■ *Raising the soil level*

Exactly how high the rock garden or bed is raised above ground level is not too vital, and it does depend to a large degree upon how much extra soil you can lay your hands on, and how much you are prepared to add in the way of peat and suchlike bulky soil-improving stuff. Even just a few inches will help to improve the drainage somewhat, although ideally you should aim for at least 30 cm (1 ft). As a general rule, the more clayey and badly drained your garden soil, the higher you should try to raise the level of the rock garden or bed; and, naturally, the lighter and better drained the garden soil, the less you will need to add height to ensure suitable conditions for miniature plants.

Additional top-soil may be bought in to build up rock gardens and raised beds but should always be carefully checked for quality and for weed roots before use. Make sure that it is good crumbly soil free from lumps of clay sub-soil or other rubbish, and take care to remove all weed roots, particularly those of troublesome weeds such as couch grass, dandelion and dock, which will cause serious problems if they become established amongst miniature plants.

It is less expensive to look for sources of extra soil from within the garden. You may be able to obtain this from excavations for paths, patios, driveways etc., especially in a new garden. It certainly makes sense not to waste good soil by laying paving, concrete or gravel over it; much better to make use of the top-soil and lay out hard-surfaced areas on more solid foundations of rubble, hardcore, sand etc. Indeed, even just the soil taken from excavating and laying a path around the rock garden or bed itself will help in building up the level of your miniature garden.

■ *The site*

Before starting any soil preparation or construction, however, choose the site for your rock garden or raised bed with care, taking into account the likes and dislikes of the plants you will be growing on it.

The vast majority of small and miniature plants, including most alpines, like a sunny site. So avoid very shady situations unless you are planning a bed specifically for plants which enjoy some shade, such as dwarf rhododendrons and azaleas. Try also to avoid very windy situations, choosing a fairly sheltered spot for preference, since many small plants are susceptible to damage from drying winds in hot weather. Dripping rain from overhead branches in winter and soggy fallen leaves in autumn are other hazards which can quickly kill off miniature plants, so sites very close to or beneath trees are not ideal either.

□ Rock garden construction □

Once you have chosen your site, soil preparation and improvement is the first and most essential step in constructing a rock garden. It should be carried out as thoroughly as possible, because it is on this, above all else, that the success or failure of the plants will depend.

■ *Soil preparation*

If your garden soil is at all heavy or clayey, it should be mixed with at least an equal amount, by bulk, of grit or stone chippings. On lighter, better-drained soils you can get away with a little less in the way of grit or chippings than a half-and-half mix, and very sandy or gravelly soils which are naturally extremely free-draining will require very little or none at all. To your mixture you should then add not less than a quarter its bulk of peat or other soil-lightening humus materials (garden compost, leafmould etc.)

These are only very rough guidelines and you really need to go by the look and feel of your individual garden soil. As a rule-of-thumb, the final planting mixture should feel very gritty and 'crunchy' when squeezed in your hand, and a moist handful should break apart and crumble very easily after squeezing. Another quick test is to dampen the soil mixture, then pour a can of water onto one spot and see whether it soaks away quickly without leaving a puddle; if it doesn't, then more than likely you will have to add more of the drainage-improving materials mentioned above.

The soil on rock gardens and raised beds should be top-dressed with stone chippings, and rocks should be placed to look like a natural outcrop.

Be sure to remove any weed roots that you may come across during soil preparation, especially those of deep-rooters like bindweed, dandelion and dock, and fast-spreaders such as couch grass and ground elder. These are a real menace in a rock garden and they can prove extremely difficult to weed out later on without seriously disturbing your tiny rock plants. Remember that even small pieces of root from stubborn weeds like these may grow away again if left in the soil, so take the greatest care to get out every scrap.

■ *Construction*

As for the actual construction of the rock garden, bear in mind that the aim should be to create, as far as possible, the impression of a natural outcrop of rocks breaking up through the soil. To this end, a few large rocks carefully arranged will always look much more effective than a scattering of smaller ones.

Form the soil into a mound with slopes which are not too steep, otherwise the soil will tend to wash down in heavy rainstorms, exposing the roots of higher plants and swamping lower ones. As a general rule, for every 30 cm (1 ft) in height, the rock garden will need to be about 1.2–1.5 m (4–5 ft) wide at the base to ensure that you get roughly the ideal angle of slope.

At this stage, you can further ensure good soil drainage and also help to build up the height of the rock garden by using stones, broken bricks, lumps of concrete, or any other such rubble as you might have lying around, to make a core over which the soil mixture may be mounded. However, if you do follow this course, take care to fill the gaps between the pieces of rubble with soil mixture; otherwise, you will leave air pockets which may cause soil subsidence and serious root disturbance later on.

The base of the soil mound can be whatever shape fits the particular situation. However, an informal outline with irregular curving edges will lend the rock garden a rather more natural appearance than a straight-edged and square-cornered rectangle or a perfect circle. If you do go for a rectangular shape, try not to make the edges too ruler-straight nor all the corners sharp right-angles. Working some gentle curves into the lines of the edges and/or breaking up their straightness with rocks, plus rounding-off the corners and varying their angles, will help in getting away from a too-formal and artificial square box-shape.

If you are building a small rock garden with the soil rising up to a single peak, it is best not to have the highest point in the exact centre, which always looks a little artificial. A more pleasing and natural effect will be achieved if the crest is offset from centre, giving longer and more gentle slopes to one side and contrasting slightly steeper slopes to the other. Probably about one-third of the way along and across the rock garden is ideal, although there is no need to be exact about this. A larger rock garden may, of course, be mounded up into a number of peaks or ridges, with gently dipping 'valleys' between.

Note that the steeper slopes of the rock garden should preferably be contrived so as to face away from the sunniest southerly aspect. They will then provide the shadiest and coolest possible planting sites for those rock plants which the reference books and nursery catalogues inform you prefer not to catch too much summer sun. Very steep slopes facing south, on the other hand, may tend to be too sun-scorched and parched in summer even to suit many alpines.

SLOPING SITES   Much of this advice assumes that you are creating a rock garden on a fairly level site, which is the commonest garden situation. On a sloping site, you will obviously be able to use the natural incline of the ground to construct an attractive rock garden without a great deal of need (or no need at all) for artificial soil mounding. More importantly, the natural drainage on a sloping site is generally far better than on a flat site. So soil mounding for improved drainage should equally be unnecessary, provided the slope is steep enough to ensure fast-draining conditions. You may also not need to add quite as much in the way of grit or chippings as on a level site, although where the soil is heavy or clayey you should still not skimp on these drainage-improving materials.

Remember that a very sunny, south-facing slope will be much hotter and drier in spring and summer than slopes facing north, east or west. In this situation, take care to add a very generous helping of humus materials to the soil, to help retain summer moisture and prevent the roots of tiny rock plants becoming too parched in dry weather.

For the same reasons, you will need to take special care on a south-facing slope to contrive shadier spots within the rock garden (by means of localized soil landscaping and thoughtful placement of rocks) if you plan to include plants which do not enjoy too much sun.

SPECIAL SOIL MIXES   Once the basic soil improvement and shaping is complete, you may wish to create pockets of varying soil mixes to cater for the special needs of different types of plant.

You will discover from specialist catalogues and reference books that some of the loveliest high-alpine plants demand exceptionally stony free-draining 'scree'-type soil conditions. If you want to try your hand with some of these, it is wise to make up special areas for them on the higher reaches of the rock garden, adding an extra dose of grit or stone chippings, plus a little more in the way of soil-improving humus material (peat, etc.)

On the other hand, some plants (usually those which prefer some shade) enjoy rather moister – though well-drained – conditions than the average run of rock plants. For these, areas of soil on the shadier slopes of the rock garden may be enriched with additional humus material to retain a little more moisture during dry spells in spring and summer.

Yet other plants must have lime-free conditions, and if your garden soil is at all limy then you will have to create pockets of non-limy planting mixture to please them. The simplest method is to make up a mix (by bulk) of two-thirds lime-free 'ericaceous'-type peat compost (available from most garden centres) to one-third lime-free grit, chippings or coarse sand. Alternatively, plain garden peat may be used in the mix instead of the lime-free peat compost; but in this case, do remember to add a dose of a non-limy compound fertilizer (such as John Innes base fertilizer) since pure peat contains virtually no plant foods. This works out somewhat cheaper than buying special ericaceous compost, especially for larger areas.

Try to make any such patch of lime-free planting mixture as large as possible, since a small area may quickly become impregnated with lime washed in from the surrounding soil. Slates, old tiles or some other water-retarding barrier buried around the edges (but not the bottom) will help to prevent this. Take care to make your pocket of lime-free mixture deep as well as wide, so that the roots of the plants will not readily grow down into the limy soil below. And remember that if your tapwater is limy then you should use rainwater (which is non-limy) for watering this area of the rock garden.

THE ROCKWORK Next, we come to the choice and positioning of the rocks. Limestones and sandstones are the traditional favourites for rock garden construction. They weather attractively, quickly developing coatings of lichen and moss which lend the rockwork an aged appearance. But find out what is available from nearby quarries, because a local stone will always work out cheaper and look more at home in your garden than stone imported from outside your area. Never mix different types of rock, and do not be tempted into thinking that lumps of concrete or suchlike rubble that you may have lying around will look just as good as proper rockwork (they won't).

In order to create the impression of a natural outcrop, the rocks should appear to emerge from the soil as though they were the tips of a much larger rock formation below ground, exposed by the weathering-away of the soil cover (Fig. 1). They should never be simply laid flat on the surface.

Where the rock garden has been mounded up on a level site, the rocks should be tilted backwards with their upper surfaces slanting down into the soil behind (Fig. 2). On a steeply sloping site, they will need to be tilted rather less, or not at all, to produce the same effect. In either case, it is vital that the back edge of each rock is buried slightly beneath soil level; otherwise the illusion that they continue below ground, as part of a large rock mass, will be shattered. This will inevitably mean that a sizeable proportion of the bulk of each rock will be buried out of sight, which may seem a waste of your valuable

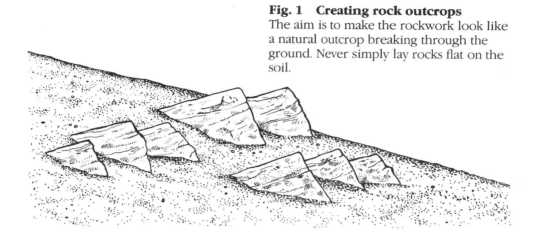

Fig. 1   Creating rock outcrops
The aim is to make the rockwork look like a natural outcrop breaking through the ground. Never simply lay rocks flat on the soil.

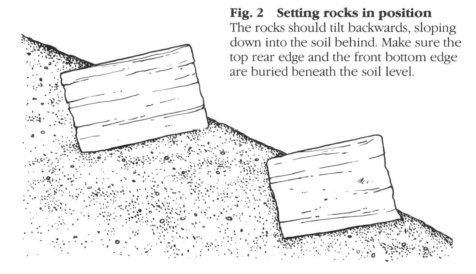

Fig. 2   Setting rocks in position
The rocks should tilt backwards, sloping down into the soil behind. Make sure the top rear edge and the front bottom edge are buried beneath the soil level.

stone but it cannot be helped if a natural effect is to be achieved.

The rocks on any one slope or side of the rock garden must all tilt in the same direction and at the same angle, as they would in a real outcrop. Group them together in roughly horizontal lines across the slope to create a series of terraces rising up to a topmost plateau or rocky summit, which will always produce a far more natural and attractive result than simply dotting single rocks around the slope. Remember also (and this is vital) that if the rocks have distinct strata lines, as many types do, then the stone should be positioned so that these lines run across the face of the rock from side to side, never vertically up and down the face nor across the top.

Crevices between neighbouring rocks should be packed with soil to provide homes for plants which, as they grow, will fill the cracks and increase the illusion of one continuous rock mass. These also provide excellent, very free-draining and sheltered planting sites for those high-alpine plants which demand such conditions. The impression of a large rock mass may further be increased by placing rocks atop one another, again with a layer of soil for planting sandwiched in between. Indeed, this is one way in which smaller rocks may be welded together to form a more impressive outcrop effect.

Make sure that the rocks are very firmly seated, so that they may be stepped on without wobbling. It is a good idea to bed them on some coarse sand (or better still, a layer of chippings topped with a layer of sand). This is not essential, but it has the added benefit of discouraging slugs and snails from nestling in the cool, moist conditions beneath the rockwork. In any case, you should ensure that you do not leave air pockets under rocks, which will provide ideal hiding places for these pests (they can very quickly do terrible damage to tiny rock plants). For the same reason, and to give the rocks further stability, pack soil firmly behind and around each rock, taking care not to leave air pockets here either.

SOIL SETTLING AND TOP DRESSING   Once construction is complete, leave the soil to settle for a week or so. This requires patience when what you really want to do is get straight on with planting, but it is essential because soil levels may need adjusting after settling, and this might well mean disturbing any plants that you may have hastily put in. Fill in with additional planting mixture any hollows which appear after settling, and take special care to top-up soil around rocks if it has settled so much that the edges which should be buried have become exposed.

Finally, spread a top-dressing of stone chippings over the soil to a depth of about 1 cm (½ in), and the garden is ready for planting. This will help to keep the plants' roots cool and moist in the fast-draining soil mixture during hot, dry spells in spring and summer, while preventing the necks of the plants (the point where many alpines are most prone to rotting-off in damp weather) from becoming too wet during autumn and winter.

Additionally, the chippings will prevent soil splashing up onto small rock plants in heavy rain, which can lead to further problems with rotting and spoil the delicate flowers of low-growing plants. It will also, to some degree, discourage weeds from seeding into the rock garden; although it will not stop established perennial weed roots already in the soil from sprouting and growing. Beware, of course, of top-dressing areas where lime-hating plants are to be planted with limestone chippings. These parts should have a layer of non-limy chippings.

■ *The surroundings*

As for the surroundings of the rock garden, much will depend on the site you have chosen. If the rock garden is surrounded by or bordering a lawn, having the grass growing up to the bases of the lowest edging rockwork does look very effective and natural. But this can make mowing a fiddly job, and plants growing around the edges will resent competing with over-long grass and being repeatedly damaged by mower blades.

A more practical alternative is to border the rock garden with a path, or at least, for ease of maintenance, with a chippings-filled channel dividing the grass from the lower rockwork and plants. Bear in mind, too, what I mentioned in the introduction to this chapter: that excavating the ground alongside the rock garden site in preparation for laying a path will, at the same time, provide you with extra material to help build up the soil level for your rock plants.

The rock garden may, of course, be linked to other miniature-gardening features which will harmonize attractively with it. For example, it could merge (preferably at the base of a shady slope) with a peat bed for small lime-hating

Even low raised beds will provide miniature plants, such as alpines, with the well-drained soil conditions they enjoy.

and moisture-loving plants. On another side, it might blend into a conifer-and-heather bed or a paved area (such as a patio) with low-growing plants spreading along the cracks and gaps between the paving (any path bordering the rock garden, whether paved or gravelled, may similarly be adorned with miniature plants and made into an additional feature). Alternatively, a section of the lower rockwork may form a handsome backdrop and edging to a small pool stocked with miniature aquatics and small bog plants.

Even an adjoining area of grass may be utilized to good effect in a way that will complement and enhance the rock garden. By naturalizing dwarf bulbs in the turf (or at least in part of it) you can create a miniature 'alpine lawn' type feature at the foot of the rock garden which will provide additional colour and interest during spring (and in autumn, too, if you choose bulbs to flower in both seasons). The only drawback is having to mow around the bulb leaves for a while during spring and early summer, but this is a small price to pay for what can be a truly charming effect (see also Chapter 7).

□ Raised bed and wall garden construction □

Just as with the rock garden, the first essential in the making of a raised bed to grow miniature plants is thorough soil preparation and improvement; the advice given earlier under 'Rock garden construction' should be followed equally diligently here.

To ensure further good drainage and to help build up the soil level of the raised bed, the top-soil on the site may be dug out and the hole filled up again with stones, broken bricks, concrete lumps and suchlike rubble. As when building a rock garden over a rubble base, however, do take care to fill with soil any air pockets amongst this drainage material to avoid subsidence problems later on. And, again just as in rock garden construction, remember that excavating and laying a path alongside or around the raised bed site will also give you valuable additional soil for use in the bed.

The raised bed may be built out from an existing garden wall (preferably in a matching building material) which will save on cost since you will only need to construct the front and sides, or it may of course be free-standing within the garden. You can make the bed any length you like, but it should not be so wide that you will have difficulty reaching into the centre for planting and maintenance. Ideal widths which will allow you to work on the middle of the bed from the side in comfort are: about 75 cm (2½ ft) for a bed built out from a tall garden wall where you will only be able to work from the one side, and 1.2–1.5 m (4–5 ft) for a free-standing bed which can be worked on from both sides.

Exactly what height you make the bed is not vital, just so long as it is raised enough to provide free-draining soil conditions for the small plants. The heavier and slower-draining the garden soil, the more advisable it is to increase the height as much as possible, while on lighter soils you can obviously get away with rather less height, if you wish. Even just a few inches will help to improve the drainage, but you should really aim for at least a foot, and about 45–60 cm (1½–2 ft) should ensure excellent drainage and prove a handy height for weeding and other maintenance work without too much bending.

Indeed, one of the great side-benefits of raised bed gardening is being able to sit in reasonable comfort on the wall of the bed and work on it (or simply admire the plants at close quarters) without needing to bend or kneel. This, incidentally, makes raised beds an ideal form of gardening for elderly and disabled gardeners who can, if necessary, work on the bed from the comfort of a chair.

In practice, of course, the height of the bed may well have to be decided largely on the basis of how much extra soil you can lay your hands on for the in-filling and/or how much additional filling material you are prepared to buy-in (not to mention the cost of building materials).

■ *Construction materials and methods*

A wide range of different materials may be used to construct raised beds; natural stone, reconstructed stone blocks, brick, up-ended concrete slabs, heavy timber, etc.

DRY-STONE BEDS Most attractive of all, and most traditional, are raised beds built with walling stone laid dry (without mortar). Quite apart from the unrivalled beauty of the natural stone, this kind of bed offers the gardener the ideal opportunity for creating fascinating and beautiful wall garden features by planting in the crevices of the stonework around the walls, adding a whole new dimension to the attractions of the raised bed. The combination of lichen- and moss-covered stone with trailing and rosette-forming miniature plants produces such an enchanting effect that it really is well worth considering this type of construction, even though natural stone is expensive.

Dry stone walls can prove a little more tricky to build than brick or block walls, and it is wise to put in some practice first, laying a small section of wall, taking it down and rebuilding until you are sure that you have acquired the knack (specialist books on dry stone wall laying are generally available through

Fig. 3   Raised bed construction

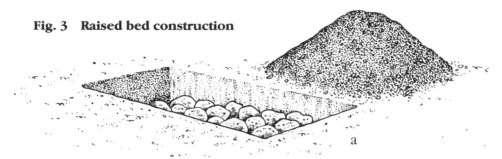

(a)   Excavate the site for the raised bed, fill the hole with drainage material, and improve the soil with peat and grit or chippings.

(b)   Be sure to leave gaps for planting in the walls of the bed, and add further drainage material in the base before filling with soil.

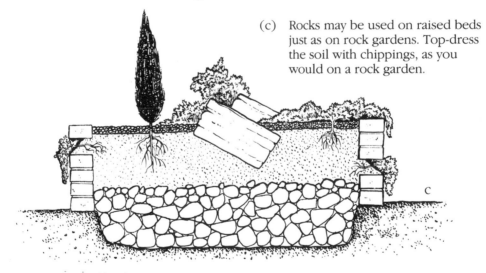

(c)   Rocks may be used on raised beds just as on rock gardens. Top-dress the soil with chippings, as you would on a rock garden.

libraries, if you want to be really certain of making a good job of it).

Use your prepared soil mixture in thin layers between the stones in place of mortar, and contrive wider crevices and gaps here and there for planting. Remember to plant these gaps as you build, because it will prove much more difficult to do this successfully once the walls are complete. Most important of all, be sure to construct the walls with a slight inwards 'batter', leaning in against the weight of the soil which the bed will contain; otherwise they may tend to sag outwards as time goes on, or may even collapse. As a rule-of-thumb, for every 30 cm (1 ft) of height that you build to, the wall should lean in at the top by about 4 cm (1½ in).

BRICKS, BLOCKS AND SLABS   If you are building with brick or blocks, you should leave gaps the size of a brick-end, staggered at varying levels around the faces of the walls, for planting purposes (Fig. 3). This will serve a double purpose: allowing you to create pretty wall gardens and, at the same time, helping to disguise the harshness of new bricks or blocks with a camouflage of plant foliage.

Up-ended slabs offer the simplest form of construction but are not the most attractive material to use. They suit best a modern style of patio garden or a paved yard, though even here there are more interesting and handsome choices that you can make. If you do use slabs, you will have to bury at least a third of their height below ground for stability. And to ensure further that they do not move outwards under the pressure of the soil behind, pack stones or other rubble hard against the bottom edge inside the bed.

Low stone, brick or block walls for small raised beds should not need a great deal in the way of foundations, and it will usually suffice to consolidate thoroughly the ground and half-bury the first course. However, the larger the bed and the taller the walls, the more advisable it is to set the bottom course onto a bed of hardcore and concrete for assured stability.

The most usual and convenient shape for a raised bed is roughly rectangular, and if you are building with brick, blocks or slabs then you will, to a large degree, be limited to fairly formal outlines. Creating brick or blockwork walls with gentle curves is possible but does demand a reasonable amount of skill if it is to look right, so this is probably best left to the experts. Dry stone beds, on the other hand, are just about as easy to construct with curving walls and rounded corners as with straight lines and squared-off corners; and they do look particularly attractive when designed to an informal shape, in the same way as a rock garden.

Before filling with planting mixture, first make sure that the drainage in the base of the raised bed is extra good. If you have not previously excavated the site and in-filled the hole with rubble, then at least thoroughly break up the ground inside the bed with a garden fork. Roughly the first third of the bed's depth should ideally then be filled with coarse drainage material such as stones, broken bricks, etc. And, as I have mentioned before, take care to fill with soil any large air pockets amongst this rubble, to prevent subsidence problems cropping up later.

■ Soil and rocks

The soil mixtures recommended earlier for rock gardens will serve just as well for raised beds. Alternatively, you can fill the bed with bought-in potting compost to which between a third and half of its bulk of grit or stone chippings has been added.

As with the rock garden, you may wish to vary the soil mixture from one area of the bed to another, to suit different types of plant, i.e. a stonier section for high-alpines which need 'scree' conditions, more humus material for plants which like moister soil, and perhaps a corner filled with a mix of ericaceous peat compost and grit or chippings for lime-hating plants, if your garden soil is too limy for these.

Where space permits, a series of raised beds may be constructed with a different soil mix in each; gritty soil in a sunny site for the general run of miniature plants, a peatier mix in a shadier spot for moisture-loving and shade-loving plants, and a bed of non-limy mixture (again in a shadier corner) for

Alpine phloxes provide bright sheets of late spring/early summer colour where there is space for them to spread.

those old favourites rhododendrons, and suchlike lime-haters.

Rocks may be used on raised beds in much the same way as on a rock garden. However, it is not advisable (nor possible) to mound the soil up too much on a small raised bed. Apart from anything else, this can cause excessive rainwater run-off and make an already extremely well-drained bed very dry in spring and summer. A little gentle mounding and shaping of the soil here and there for landscape effect on a large bed is all right, but the soil in a small bed should really be fairly level. This means that the rocks will have to rise out of the soil mixture tilted back at a steep angle to achieve the look of a natural outcrop (see p. 20). Of course, you can grow miniature plants perfectly well in a raised bed without any rockwork at all, but one or two rocks do add greatly to the miniature landscape effect.

Finally, leave the soil mixture to settle for a week or two, top-up if necessary, and then top-dress the bed with a 1 cm (½ in) deep layer of stone chippings as recommended for rock gardens. Remember that beds, or parts of beds, intended for lime-hating plants should not be top-dressed with limestone chippings.

■ *Wall gardens*

The raised bed offers the gardener one situation where wall gardens can be created very easily, but naturally any retaining wall with suitable gaps for planting may be turned into an attractive feature.

Existing dry-stone retaining walls (should you be lucky enough to have one in or bordering the garden) are the most obvious choice with their ready-made crevices. If the gaps are rather small for easy planting, you may be able to carefully prise out the odd small stone to make a decent planting hole, provided you make sure that there is a larger stone remaining above to bridge the gap and prevent a collapse. Existing cemented retaining walls may seem an impossible proposition; but even here it may be possible, with a lot of patience plus a hammer and chisel, to cut out the occasional planting hole to brighten up the wall.

If you are planning a new retaining wall to hold up a bank of soil or to create a terrace on a sloping site, then you can of course build in planting holes as suggested for raised beds. Bear in mind, however, that a wall intended to retain a great weight of soil in this sort of situation will have to be more strongly constructed and be given more solid foundations than for a raised bed. So do seek expert advice and help, especially if the wall is to be any great height. And if you do get a builder in to carry out the work, do remind him that you would like some planting holes left in the wall.

Remember also to fill in behind your retaining wall with a free-draining and humus-rich soil mixture for the wall plants to get their roots into. Do not simply shovel back any old hotch-potch of unimproved top-soil, useless sub-soil, stones, etc. that the building work may have thrown up.

□ Planting and maintenance □

Rock plants, dwarf conifers and miniature shrubs are all invariably pot-grown by nurserymen so may, in theory, be planted at virtually any time of year when the soil is not frozen solid.

In practice, the best times to plant are in spring and late summer to early autumn. Try, if possible, to avoid the hottest months of mid-summer, when these kinds of small plants may struggle to become established if the weather turns dry. Late autumn and winter planting, when the soil is cold and wet, is not recommended either. Keep well watered during hot or dry spells after planting; and if the plants start to suffer during a prolonged period of scorching weather, providing temporary shade will aid recovery (an up-turned flower pot or bucket popped over a small plant will do the trick in an emergency, and can make the difference between survival or loss in really hot weather).

Spring-flowering miniature bulbs are planted in autumn, of course, and dwarf autumn-flowering bulbs are sent out by bulb nurseries and available from garden centres for planting in late summer.

■ *Planting techniques*

Planting methods are the same for rock gardens and raised beds. Water the plants in their pots then carefully tap them out, trying not to break up the root ball. If long roots have wound themselves around and around the inside or bottom of the pot, then some of these may be gently 'teased' loose to encourage them to grow out into the new planting mixture. Apart from this, for general planting purposes, the ball of soil and roots should be disturbed as little as possible.

Having moved the stone chippings away from the intended planting hole, take care to plant to the same depth as the soil in the pot, lightly firming the new soil mixture around the root ball with your fingers. Spread your top-dressing of stone chippings back around the necks of the plants, being careful to get the layer of chippings right under the foliage of low-growing and trailing plants (Fig. 4), then water-in thoroughly.

Gaps between rocks and in wall gardens are best planted as you build the rockwork or wall, since it is always somewhat easier to get the plants snugly tucked into their tight-fitting homes at this stage, especially where small crevices are concerned. If the holes are largish ones, then planting after construction is quite possible but can prove a slightly more fiddly job.

Make sure that the roots of the plant are in good contact with the soil at the back of the planting hole or crevice and firmly pack soil mixture around the root to fill up the gap, taking great care not to leave any air pockets. With vertical crevices and planting holes, it is always a good idea to wedge some small stones into the front, around the neck of the plant. This should help prevent the soil from washing out.

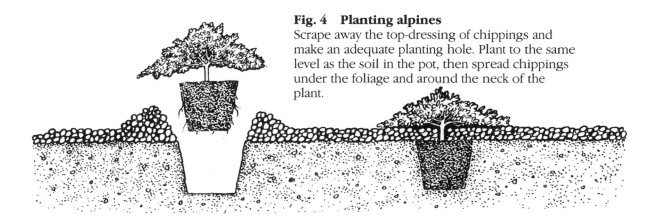

Fig. 4 Planting alpines
Scrape away the top-dressing of chippings and make an adequate planting hole. Plant to the same level as the soil in the pot, then spread chippings under the foliage and around the neck of the plant.

Fig. 5   Planting in rock crevices
Plants for narrow rock crevices may have some of the soil carefully shaken or rinsed off the root ball, so that the roots may be spread out in the crevice and packed around with soil.

When faced with a very narrow crevice, you can gently shake or wash some of the soil off the roots, so that they may be spread out in the crack and packed around with soil (Fig. 5). Alternatively, small rooted cuttings or seedlings may easily be inserted into the tiniest of spaces.

Do not forget that this type of situation particularly suits rosette-forming plants and those alpines which enjoy extra-good soil drainage and some protection from winter damp (specialist nursery catalogues and reference books will tell you which these are). Planting sites tucked in close to the base of a large rock are also well sheltered, dryish situations which will please the fussier rock plants.

■ *Overcrowding problems*
Try to resist the temptation to over-plant the rock garden or raised bed. Cramming too many plants into a small area, without making full allowance for their future growth and ultimate size, is a common mistake. It will only lead to heartache and extra work later on when you are faced with the inevitable problems of overcrowded plantings. Remember also to avoid placing tiny slow-growing plants which form tight cushions or tufts too close to strong-growing and fast-spreading plants; otherwise constant cutting-back (or eventual replanting) will be necessary to stop the smaller plants being swamped.

Indeed, if the rock garden or raised bed is a very small one then you should really avoid altogether the more rampant rock plants, such as the popular aubrietas and helianthemums, and the faster-growing dwarf conifers and rock shrubs. Go instead for the neater high-alpines and the very slowest-growing trees and shrubs, which are unlikely to get out of hand even in the most restricted of spaces. Quite apart from causing fewer overcrowding problems, these daintier treasures will provide you with a great deal more variety and interest from a small area than a lesser number of more space-hungry plants.

If you are planning to include some fast-spreading plants for quick effect, aim to put these where they will pose the least possible threat to smaller plants, hemmed in between rocks or tucked into a corner of the rock garden or bed, where they can be trained to trail harmlessly outwards. Be particularly wary of plants which nursery catalogues and reference books describe as spreading quickly by underground runners. These can very soon take over large areas and prove absolute murder to weed out. They should be isolated in a corner

Opposite: *Alpine campanulas are valuable for masses of bright blue flowers throughout summer.*

cut off from the rest of the planting mixture by rocks set deep below the surface; or else they should be banned entirely, especially in a very small rock garden or bed.

■ *Maintenance*

One of the most important aspects of rock garden and raised bed maintenance after planting is regular weeding, since fast-growing weeds can quickly smother the tinier plants. Aim to remove weed seedlings as soon as they appear and before they get so large that extracting them will threaten to disturb the roots of small plants, especially if they pop up in the middle of a tight cushion of rock plant foliage (which weed seedlings have a nasty habit of doing). Dead autumn leaves from nearby trees or shrubs must also be removed as quickly as possible. If left to lie and turn soggy, they too will smother small plants, causing them to rot.

Do not be misled by the need for fast-draining soil into thinking that the plants will positively revel in drought conditions once established. The aim of giving them a well-drained soil mixture is to prevent their roots becoming waterlogged and rotting-off in wet weather, particularly during winter; not to keep them bone-dry.

Water frequently and thoroughly if the weather turns hot and dry during the growing season; most importantly, in late spring and early summer, which is when most plants of mountain origin put on a fast spurt of growth and expect to be naturally well watered by run-off from melting snowfields. With the approach of late summer and autumn, the need for heavy watering generally diminishes as the plants' growth slows down after flowering.

Miniature plants do not require heavy feeding, which tends to encourage leafy growth at the expense of flowers. A scattering of a slow-acting compound organic fertilizer as a top-dressing applied in late winter or early spring is quite adequate. John Innes base fertilizer is ideal for this purpose and is suitable as a general feed for all miniature plants, including lime-haters. On lime-hating plants do not use bonemeal (which is limy) or fertilizers containing bonemeal.

At the same time, if you can manage it, replenish the top-dressing of stone chippings as these tend to work their way down into the soil mixture over a period of time. Pay special attention to topping-up around the necks of the plants, and on the steeper slopes where the chippings layer is most likely to have worn thin.

□ Planting design □

The majority of rock plants flower during spring, so it is easy to have a colourful display on the rock garden or raised bed at this time of year. However, what you should be aiming for is not just a stunning spring show but a succession of colour and interest throughout the seasons.

Planting suggestions for different times of the year are given in Chapter 3, and these should help you to balance your planting scheme to avoid seasonal dull spots. Summer is not too difficult, as there are a number of popular rock plants which bloom continuously over a long period through the midsummer months and provide a very useful backbone to the display at this time. Autumn and winter are rather less easy, but even these dull seasons may be brightened up with the help of a few invaluable and dependable plants and bulbs.

Remember that evergreen plants, shrubs and conifers with colourful foliage tints are useful for adding interest to the rock garden or raised bed all year round, and especially in winter when flowers are scarce.

Many alpines have attractive grey or silvery leaves and these, along with the brighter foliage hues of other plants, will provide interesting contrasts against the general greenery on the rock garden or bed. But do not just let these contrasts happen by chance; try to plan your planting scheme so that you create the maximum visual impact by juxtaposing not only plants with different foliage colours, but also plants with widely different leaf shapes and growth habits.

■ The layout

The first stage in planning your planting scheme is to decide where the largest 'architectural' plants, the conifers, dwarf deciduous trees and shrubs, are to go. These lend your miniature garden or landscape the essential elements of height and bulk just as larger trees and shrubs do in general garden planting and in attractive natural landscapes. Without a good framework of these taller and bulkier plants, the end result will appear rather flat and uninteresting.

Next in terms of scale come the bushier and more upright plants; then there are those which form low-growing mats of trailing stems or wide-spreading underground shoots, and finally the daintiest little alpines which restrict themselves to tight cushions and hummocks of foliage studded with flowers, or handsome clusters of rosette-shaped leaves.

The basic planting plan should be to place the majority of the taller and bulkier trees, shrubs and plants towards the middle or back of the rock garden or raised bed, generally grading down to smaller and smaller plants as you move out towards the edges. This is much the same way that you would plant an ordinary garden border or bed. It is also a fair imitation of a natural landscape, where forests and woods of tall trees gradually give way to lower-growing shrubs and then to grasses and other smaller plants.

Of course, this is only a very basic framework which should not be followed too religiously. Here and there you should create some contrasts of height and scale to catch the eye and add interest to the layout; a solitary tall, columnar conifer rising out of a carpet of low-spreading plants, for example.

■ Placing the plants

Those plants which form clusters of rosettes or tight cushions and hummocks look particularly good planted in crevices between rocks, where they will slowly spread to fill the gaps and weld the rockwork together. These types also look very handsome, and will be well sheltered from wet winter weather, tucked in close to the base of a rock. In this situation they will tend to creep up the rockface slightly, as well as along its base, producing a charming effect.

Trailing plants placed behind rocks will spread over the top of the rockwork and cascade very attractively down the rockface. These play an especially important role in raised-bed gardening, planted around the edges to spill over and down the walls. Apart from adding an extra dimension to the raised-bed planting scheme, these trailers help to soften the harshness of newly-built walls until the building materials weather and mellow. They are most valuable for this purpose where less attractive materials, such as up-ended concrete paving slabs, have been used for the walls. And planted in corners of the raised bed, they will also help to camouflage the unnatural sharpness and formality of corners where brick, blockwork or slab walls meet at right-angles.

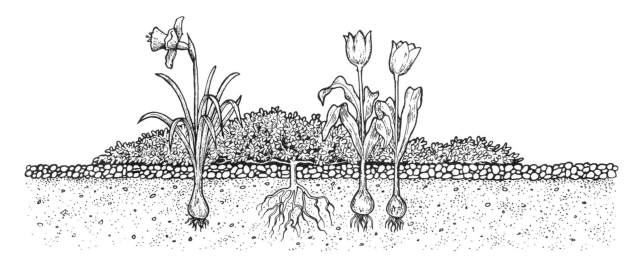

Fig. 6 Underplanting with dwarf bulbs
Low mat-forming and trailing plants may be underplanted with miniature bulbs for extra seasonal colour.

Of course, planting holes and crevices in the walls of the raised bed (and in other retaining walls) equally cry out for trailing plants; and for rosette-forming plants, which look just right in such a situation and will greatly appreciate the extra free drainage and rain shelter of a wall-garden site.

Try to ensure that there will be continuity of colour and interest throughout the seasons in all parts of the rock garden or raised bed, by mixing and blending plants for spring, summer, autumn and winter flowering.

Miniature bulbs are extremely useful for squeezing in additional colour, since they may be popped into small gaps alongside or between low-growing plants. If trailing shoots eventually cover their planting site, the bulbs will not mind too much, simply spearing up through the mat of rock plant foliage in their due season and then dying down again. This, in effect, gives the gardener double value, allowing plants for one season and dwarf bulbs for another to be accommodated in the same growing space (Fig. 6).

One slight drawback with this is that slugs and snails sheltering in the cool, shady conditions beneath the mat of rock plant foliage may attack the fleshy bulb shoots as they appear. So do keep an eye out for this kind of damage and deal quickly with these pests if it should occur.

Another disadvantage is that most dwarf bulbs like to be fairly dry during their summer rest period. Constant watering of the covering rock plants may, eventually, shorten the bulbs' lives so that they might have to be replaced over a period of time. Where they are covered by trailing shoots this is not too difficult; simply a matter of carefully lifting the foliage cover and planting fresh bulbs, taking care not to disturb the plant roots too much. Mixing some additional coarse sand or grit into the soil where miniature bulbs are to be planted will help to ensure drier summer conditions for them and prolong their lives.

Plants which offer more than one feature, such as flowers plus colourful foliage, or flowers followed by handsome seed heads, give good value for growing space on a small rock garden or raised bed, so seek these out in nursery catalogues.

PLANTS FOR ROCK GARDENS AND RAISED BEDS

Few of the miniature plants, bulbs, shrubs and trees described here are particularly difficult to grow. Indeed, the majority are quite easy, given the well-drained soil conditions of a rock garden or raised bed, and will thrive without a great deal of fuss or attention, while many are strong-growing enough even for an ordinary garden border (see Chapter 5).

Some do have special needs, such as lime-free soil. And one or two, notably the beautiful lime-hating autumn gentians, can prove more of a challenge than the rest. But even these are not especially difficult, provided their basic (and fairly straightforward) requirements are catered for.

□ Trees □

Unfortunately there are nowhere near as many truly miniature deciduous trees as there are dwarf conifers for the gardener to choose from. However, one or two dainty beauties suitable for rock gardens and raised beds are available.

■ Dwarf deciduous trees
Few small trees are more elegant and refined than the lovely Japanese maples, with their multi-tiered and fan-like branchlets of deeply divided leaves in shades of green or purple-red. Famous for their fiery autumn tints, these have long been favourites among discerning gardeners.

Most will grow far too large after a few years, but as young specimens they will make a beautiful feature on a large rock garden or raised bed until they eventually have to be moved elsewhere in the garden. Unnamed seedlings offered in garden centres and catalogues, in particular, are a real gamble as there is no knowing just how fast these will shoot up. By far your best choice would be the low-growing *Acer palmatum* 'Dissectum' or *A. p.* 'Dissectum Atropurpureum'. Both have extremely finely divided, almost ferny, foliage that is green in the ordinary form, purple-red in the case of 'Dissectum Atropurpureum'.

These two delightful dwarf acers are suitable for larger rock gardens and raised beds, where they should prove slow-growing enough never to become a real problem. On a rock garden they look especially good planted where their low-spreading branches can trail down over rockwork. And on a raised bed they are best placed close to the edge or in a corner where the foliage will tumble very attractively outwards and down the wall of the bed.

For small rock gardens and beds, there is no slower-growing miniature tree than the dwarf willow *Salix* × *boydii*. Never more than about 30 cm (1 ft) tall and rather less in width even after a great many years, this little gem has all the appearance of a natural bonsai tree with its gnarled branches and tiny silvery-grey rounded leaves. You will probably have to seek it out in alpine nursery catalogues, since garden centres seldom offer it, but it is well worth the search.

The dwarf birch *Betula nana* can also be found in specialist alpine catalogues and is a charming little twiggy tree with tiny glossy-green leaves (which turn bright gold in autumn) crowding its wiry branches. The ordinary form slowly grows to 30–60 cm (1–2 ft) while the variety 'Glengarry' is the better choice where space is strictly limited, reaching only 25–30 cm (10–12 in).

■ *Dwarf coniferous trees*

Dwarf conifers are, of course, very popular choices and invaluable for creating miniature landscape effects. But not all of them are suitable for planting on smaller rock gardens and raised beds by any means. Some of the varieties commonly sold as 'slow-growng', such as *Chamaecyparis lawsoniana* 'Ellwoodii' and *C. l.* 'Ellwood's Gold', may well (as you will discover if you check with reference books) top 1.5–1.8 m (5–6 ft) eventually. And even amongst the so-called dwarf varieties there are many which will easily reach 60–90 cm (2–3 ft) in height and (much more importantly) the same in width across the base; which means they can take up quite a bit of room after a few years.

The answer is simple – always carefully check on rate of growth and ultimate size before buying, and tailor your choice carefully to the size of your miniature garden or landscape. Be extra wary of low-growing spreading conifers, as most of these will very quickly gobble up ground and become a real nuisance where space is strictly limited. The varieties of *Juniperus horizontalis* tend to be particularly vigorous spreaders, eventually covering as much as 2 m (6 ft) of ground.

TRUE MINIATURES   One of the very neatest, and most charming, of truly dwarf conifers is the diminutive *Juniperus communis* 'Compressa'. This little beauty, commonly and evocatively known as the Noah's Ark Juniper, grows into the most perfectly shaped slender spire of tightly-packed greyish green foliage. Universally acknowledged as one of the very best conifers for use in creating miniature landscapes, it is safe to plant in the smallest of rock gardens or raised beds, growing little more than an inch a year and seldom reaching much more than 60 cm (2 ft) in height. Indeed, it is one of the few dwarf conifers which is widely recommended even for the highly restricted confines of a tiny trough garden or window box.

There are a number of other very slow-growing true miniatures to look out for in garden centres and catalogues and these include:

Abies balsamea 'Hudsonia', 30 cm (1 ft), a slowly spreading bushy dwarf conifer with densely-packed dark green foliage and bright green spring shoots.

Chamaecyparis lawsoniana 'Minima Aurea', 30–60 cm (1–2 ft), one of the very best dwarf golden-foliage varieties, forming a dense conical bush which remains bright golden-yellow all year round. *C. l.* 'Pygmaea Argentea', 30–45 cm (1½–2 ft), is dark bluish-green with contrasting creamy-white tips to its shoots.

Cryptomeria japonica 'Vilmoriniana', 30–60 cm (1–2 ft), has a very tight ball of moss-like foliage, turning a rich purple-red in winter.

Juniperus squamata 'Blue Star', 25–30 cm (10–12 in), a slightly spreading low bushy conifer with an eye-catching bright steely-blue colouring; excellent as a contrast to golden varieties.

Picea abies 'Nidiformis', 30–40 cm (12–16 in), a reliably slow-spreading bushy type, eventually 45–60 cm (1½–2 ft) across.

Thuja occidentalis 'Danica', 30–45 cm (12–18 in), a neat little bush with bronze winter tints, green in summer.

LARGER CONIFERS   Rather less dwarf but suitable for larger rock gardens and raised beds are:

Chamaecyparis pisifera 'Plumosa Aurea Nana', 60 cm (2 ft), a very bright yellow, conical in shape with soft feathery foliage.

Picea glauca 'Albertiana Conica', 60–90 cm (2–3 ft), a beautiful dwarf spruce with a quite perfect conical form; bright apple-green young shoots in spring contrast vividly with the darker green of the older branches.

Taxus baccata 'Standishii', 90–120 cm (3–4 ft), a very slow-growing golden yew, making a very narrow columnar tree.

Thuja occidentalis 'Rheingold', 90 cm (3 ft), a deservedly popular conifer, a rounded cone-shape with distinctive old-gold coloured foliage in summer, turning rich copper-gold in winter. *T. o.* 'Sunkist', 75–90 cm (2½–3 ft) is similar, but keeps its bright golden colouring all year round. *T. orientalis* 'Aurea Nana', 60–75 cm, a very shapely oval bush with yellow-green summer foliage.

Note that the heights given in these conifer lists are those that can be expected after about 10 years in average growing conditions. Some may eventually grow a little larger.

FAST GROWING CONIFERS   Should you be impatient for a quick effect on the rock garden or raised bed, it is possible to plant rather faster-growing conifers than you really have room for, as a temporary measure only. But you will have to accept that these must be moved when they eventually get too large. This is not too difficult with slow-growing and dwarf conifers, which make shallow and compact root balls that may easily be lifted and moved if care is taken not to disturb the roots too much.

If you do take this easy option, then it is important, at the same time, to buy some neater dwarf conifers more suited to the size of your miniature garden or landscape, and grow these on (in pots or elsewhere in the garden) as long-term replacements. And do take care to remove the faster-growing temporary trees before they become so large that taking them out would seriously disturb surrounding plants. For easy removal, you can, of course, keep the root balls of these short-term conifers compact by digging round them annually and thereby root-pruning them. This will also slow down their growth rate.

PLANTING DESIGN Finally, a quick word on planting design specifically regarding dwarf conifers. They generally look more effective and natural planted in small groups of two or three together, rather than dotted singly, and evenly-spaced, across the rock garden or bed. These little groves may then be supplemented with the odd outlying solitary tree or two.

The groups may be made up of different varieties with contrasting foliage tints for maximum visual impact; or, where there is room to experiment with different effects, two or three trees of the same variety can provide an equally interesting and appealing, if rather more subtle, feature. The trees in the group should vary at least a little in height and outline. This is easy enough to manage with different varieties. If you fancy planting two or three of the same type together, then achieve this variety by trying to select specimens of different ages and heights from the garden centre or nursery beds.

Take care to allow enough space between the trees for future sideways growth. However, having said that, it does not really matter too much if the conifers grow into one another a little after a number of years. Provided they have enough room to develop properly in the early stages, this 'inter-growth' can look quite attractive and natural.

□ Shrubs □

One or two dwarf shrubs will always greatly enhance any rock garden or raised bed. They are as important as the conifers for adding bulk (and height, in the case of the taller types) to the miniature garden or landscape.

At the same time, broad-leaved shrubs provide a valuable contrast to the smaller-leaved conifers; so that a mini-garden which relies entirely on dwarf conifers for its bulkier architectural plants will tend to have a rather boring sameness about it, while a mix of conifers and shrubs will have more variety and visual interest.

Just as with the conifers, make sure that the shrubs you choose really are dwarf enough to suit the situation. The long-flowering shrubby potentillas, for example, are sometimes suggested as suitable choices; but most eventually grow too big for the smaller rock garden or raised bed. Ensure, also, that your soil type will suit the shrubs you pick. A number of the miniature shrubs commonly listed in the catalogues of specialist rock plant nurseries must have lime-free soil, or a lime-free peaty planting mixture if your garden soil is limy or chalky; including, of course, the many dwarf species and varieties of rhododendron.

One of the most frequently recommended and widely available shrubs for foliage effect is the silvery-grey, woolly-leaved rock willow, *Salix lanata*. But at 60–90 cm (2–3 ft) in height it is distinctly on the large side. Where space permits, it is well worth a place both for its handsome foliage and for the showy yellow catkins in spring. For small mini-gardens, however, the truly tiny silver-grey-leaved *Salix boydii*, mentioned earlier as a miniature deciduous tree, is much the safer bet.

■ Winter colour
There are colourful foliage tints of yellow and bronze-red to be found amongst the many different varieties of heather, with the bonus of flowers as well, and these are especially useful for providing interest during winter. The *Erica herbacea* (syn. *E. carnea*) varieties are the most valuable for miniature gardens,

The showy upward-facing bellflowers of Campanula carpatica *are freely produced all summer long.*

being compact and low-growing – about 25 cm (6–8 in) – and flowering over a long period throughout winter and early spring. In addition, unlike the majority of summer-flowering heathers, these do not mind limy soil. Commonly available varieties include: 'Anne Sparkes', orange-yellow foliage and purple flowers; 'Aurea', golden foliage, deep pink flowers; 'Foxhollow', gold foliage tints and pale pink flower spikes; 'Springwood Pink' and 'Springwood White', both very early-flowering varieties; and 'Vivellii', deep carmine-red flowers and handsome bronze-green foliage.

■ *Rhododendrons for spring*

While the winter-flowering heathers are invaluable for colour in the bleakest months of the year, the most desirable dwarf shrubs for the milder days of spring are undoubtedly the rhododendrons. They are not particularly difficult to grow, provided you can give them lime-free soil or a specially made-up peat planting mixture (see Chapters 2 and 6).

Even if your soil is not limy, you should still mix in an extra dose of peat to help keep these little beauties moist at the roots in dry weather. The one thing they hate almost as much as lime in the soil is prolonged drought. For this reason, they are best planted where they will receive a little shade, although most will do reasonably well in full sun if given plenty of humus in the soil and watered regularly in hot spells (with rainwater if your tapwater is limy). On the rock garden they will obviously prefer the less sun-baked conditions of a northerly slope to being on a hot, dry south slope.

There is quite a range to choose from, and most good garden centres offer at least a few. They do vary quite considerably in size, so here again (as with the dwarf conifers) select carefully to suit the scale of your miniature garden.

Some of the neatest, ideal for smaller rock gardens and raised beds, are:

Rhododendron impeditum, 20–30 cm (8–12 in), a really tiny alpine species with miniature leaves and lilac-blue flowers.

'Pink Drift', 30–45 cm (1–1½ ft), a compact bush with small leaves and masses of lavender-pink flowers.

'Carmen', 40 cm (16 in), a low-spreading variety with attractive dark glossy leaves and deep crimson waxy bells.

'Jenny', 25–30 cm (10–12 in), very prostrate and creeping habit, with large red bell flowers.

'Scarlet Wonder', 40 cm (16 in), ruby-red trumpets.

'Chikor', 35 cm (14 in), has small leaves and bright yellow flower clusters.

'Curlew', 30–45 cm (1–1½ ft), has primrose yellow bells above dark glossy foliage.

Rather taller-growing but suitable for larger rock gardens and beds:

'Blue Diamond', 60–75 cm (2–2½ ft), masses of lavender-blue funnel-shaped flowers.

'Blue Tit', 60 cm (2 ft), similar but a little slower-growing.

'Praecox', 60–90 cm (2–3 ft), a popular and easy-growing old variety, the rosy-purple funnel flowers appearing very early, from late winter onward.

'Cowslip', 50 cm (20 in), pink buds open to creamy-yellow flowers.

'Cilpinense', 60–75 cm (2–2½ ft), white bells flushed and speckled with pink.

'Elizabeth', 60 cm (2 ft), a spreading bush producing clusters of rich scarlet trumpets.

The popular dwarf evergreen azaleas tend to grow a little too large for smaller rock gardens and raised beds, and in any case their flower colourings are generally rather too bold and garish to associate well with the more refined blooms of tiny alpine plants and shrubs. A better place for these is in the peat bed (see Chapter 6) or in a tub on their own.

■ More spring colour

The cassiopes are charming and very dwarf, heather-like, spring-flowering alpine shrubs which demand the same lime-free and moist growing conditions as the rhododendrons, and which look good planted with them (as indeed do the heathers themselves). They prefer some shade, so tucking them in on the north side of a shade-throwing dwarf rhododendron is a good idea if the site is sunny. Unfortunately they are not well-known and you will generally only find them in specialist rock plant catalogues. The flowers are enchanting, purest white bells dangling elegantly from thin thread-like shoots.

Dwarf brooms are useful shrubs for spring colour and are good choices for the driest situations, being very drought tolerant. Most are low-growing spreaders and ideal for the front of the rock garden or bed.

Best known and one of the loveliest, is *Cytisus × kewensis*, with arching branches smothered in creamy flowers. This is superb planted behind rocks or at the edge of a raised bed, where it will trail and spill downwards quite spectacularly. But it can get quite big after a while, and for a small mini-garden you would do better looking for a neater type, like the tiny butter-yellow-flowered *C. ardoinii*.

For late spring and early summer there are the sweet-scented dwarf daphnes, a truly aristocratic group of little shrubs. These have long been firm favourites with rock garden enthusiasts for their neat growth habits and for the pervasiveness of their perfume, which will fill the entire garden on warm, humid days.

Daphne retusa is both one of the easiest to grow well and one of the most desirable, forming a compact mound of dark glossy leaves covered with a profusion of highly fragrant purple-flushed white star flowers. It will eventually reach 60–90 cm (2–3 ft) but only after a very lengthy period, so it should not pose a problem for quite a few years on a small rock garden or bed.

Decidedly suited to the smallest of miniature gardens is the low mat-forming *D. cneorum*. This really is one to rave over, with its ground-hugging branches, bright pink flowers and heady fragrance. Look out for the variety 'Eximia', which is a little stronger-growing, larger-flowered and more richly coloured than the ordinary form. Other species can be found in the catalogues, but this and *D. retusa* are the ones to start with.

And for a splash of warm colour in the spring miniature garden there is the delightful little *Berberis × stenophylla* 'Corallina Compacta' a 30–45 cm (12–18 in) evergreen with tiny, glossy dark green leaves and orange-yellow flowers opening from coral-red buds.

■ Non-stop summer flowers

Potentillas are valuable long-flowering shrubs for the summer months but, as I've already mentioned, most eventually grow too tall and spread too widely for all but the largest rock gardens and raised beds. The following are two of the neatest for more restricted spaces: *Potentilla arbuscula* 'Beesii', 30–40 cm (12–16 in), golden flowers produced above silvery foliage; and *P. fruticosa* 'Mandschurica', 30–45 cm (1–1½ ft), a low-spreading shrub with pure white flowers over greyish leaves. These, and all shrubby potentillas, can be restricted

Sempervivums are useful easy-growing plants for year-round foliage effects, with their handsome leaf rosettes.

somewhat by trimming back the tips of the shoots after flowering.

The helianthemums, likewise, will provide flowers all summer long but are rather fast spreaders for a small mini-garden, although here again, cutting back after flowering will help to keep them under control. Where space is at a premium, do not be tempted into planting too many of these popular, low-growing shrubs for a quick effect. Remember that you could squeeze half-a-dozen or more tiny true alpines into the same space that one helianthemum may eventually take up. Rock plant nurseries sometimes offer wild species that are neater-growing but lack the wide colour range of the more usual varieties, being generally yellow-flowered.

Summer-flowering heathers bloom over a long period but the commonest varieties (the *Calluna vulgaris* types) are too vigorous for smaller rock gardens and raised beds. Most also demand lime-free soil. The varieties of *Erica cinerea* are some of the tidiest growers, generally 15–30 cm (6–12 in) in height and spread, requiring non-limy soil but tolerating dry conditions better than most other heathers.

Widely available varieties include: 'C.D. Eason', bright red; 'Golden Drop', purple flowers and golden foliage, turning orange in winter; 'Pink Ice', a clear bright pink; and 'Purple Beauty', a very free-flowering rich purple. The flower spikes of these 'bell heathers' are particularly brilliant and rich in their colourings and last from mid-summer through to autumn. The stronger-growing *Calluna vulgaris* types, if you have room for them, will also provide valuable late-season colour, some varieties continuing virtually throughout the autumn months.

The dwarf hebes are useful evergreen shrubs for long-lasting summer flowers. Most of those offered in garden centres are small border shrubs, but the following are suitable for larger rock gardens and raised beds where there is room for them to spread: *Hebe* 'Carl Teschner', 30 cm (1 ft), spikes of violet-blue flowers all summer long; and *H. pinguifolia* 'Pagei', 15–23 cm (6–9 in), a ground-hugging mat of attractive grey-green leaves and white flowers in early summer.

Finally, one of my particular favourites is the very free-flowering *Hypericum olympicum*. This is a small shrublet often treated as a rock plant because of its rather loose-branching and low-growing habit. But if the long flowering shoots are cut hard back when the display ends each year, then it does make a compact little 15–20 cm (6–8 in) bush with greyish leaves that looks handsome all year round. The large golden-yellow, saucer-flowers are produced endlessly throughout summer.

□ Rock plants □

It is as important to tailor your choice of rock plants to the size of your miniature garden as it is with shrubs and conifers. The problem is not so much one of height (although this can be a factor) but more a question of spread and invasiveness.

Do remember that the smaller the rock garden or raised bed, the more wary you should be of introducing strong-growing everyday rock plants which may take up more space than their interest value warrants, or which may overrun tinier and more exciting treasures. Be especially cautious about plants whose reference book or catalogue descriptions include 'invasive' or 'seeds itself about freely'. These will either take over large areas by means of runners or underground shoots, or turn into troublesome weeds whose seedlings pop up all over the place. An example of a planting scheme for a small rock garden or raised bed is shown in Fig. 7.

There is no shortage of rock plants for spring flowers, and anyone can have a bright display at this time of year. But do not forget that your plant choices should contain a good balance of plants for different seasons, to ensure interest all year round.

■ *Masses of spring colour*
Probably best known of all the spring-flowering rock plants are the aubrietas. These extremely popular plants cover themselves in sheets of bright colour over a long period, but they are typical examples of the kind of plant to avoid if space is strictly limited in the miniature garden. Their fast-spreading mats, up to 60 cm (2 ft) across, make them suitable only for the larger rock garden or raised bed; or for planting in a wall, where they will cascade downwards in a blaze of red, purple, mauve or pink according to variety. If the aubrietas do threaten to get out of hand, cutting hard back after flowering will help to keep them in check (although this is the kind of chore that you should aim to avoid by choosing plants to suit the available growing space).

The yellow-flowered varieties of *Alyssum saxatile* are also popular choices for a quick mass of spring colour, and these make excellent companion plants

Fig. 7   Small rock garden example planting scheme

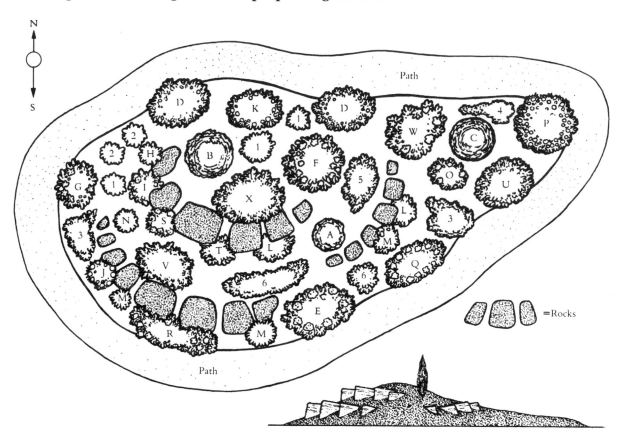

Note: This example planting scheme may be adapted for a small raised bed, with greater use of trailing plants around the edges of the bed, plus trailers and rosette-forming crevice plants in the walls.

Trees and shrubs
(A) *Juniperus communis* 'Compressa'; (B) *Abies balsamea* 'Hudsonia'; (C) *Cryptomeria japonica* 'Vilmoriniana'; (D) *Erica carnea* varieties; (E) *Daphne cneorum* 'Eximia'; (F) *D. retusa*; (G) *Hypericum olympicum*.

Plants
(H) *Ramonda myconi*; (I) *Saxifraga burseriana* 'Gloria'; (J) *S.* 'Jenkinsae'; (K) *S. oppositifolia*; (L) *Primula marginata* varieties; (M) *P. pubescens* varieties; (N) *Gentiana verna*; (O) *G. acaulis*; (P) *Phlox douglasii* variety; (Q) *Armeria caespitosa*; (R) *Campanula cochlearifolia*; (S) *Saxifraga cochlearis*; (T) *S. cotyledon* 'Southside Seedling'; (U) *Dianthus* 'La Bourbrille'; (V) *D. alpinus*; (W) *Geranium subcaulescens*; (X) *Polygonum vacciniifolium*.

Bulbs
(1) *Cyclamen coum*; (2) *C. cilicium*; (3) *Crocus chrysanthus* varieties; (4) *C. medius*; (5) *Narcissus bulbocodium*; (6) 'Reticulata' irises.

to the aubrietas (where space allows). The neatest varieties for smaller sites are 'Gold Ball', 'Compactum' and 'Flore Plenum' (double-flowered).

Arabis caucasica (syn. *A. albida*) is widely planted for its fast-spreading blanket of snow-white spring flowers but really is far too invasive for rock gardens and raised beds. However, this and the *Alyssum saxatile* varieties do (like the aubrietas) make good wall plants where a quick effect is desired. Varieties include 'Snowflake' (larger-flowered) and 'Flore Pleno' (double-flowered).

■ *True miniatures for spring*
At the very opposite end of the scale, the kabschia saxifrages are immensely neater mat and cushion plants for early spring colour, ideal for even the most restricted spaces. Their flowering season actually commences before winter is out, which makes them particularly valuable, and continues over a long period until spring has well and truly arrived. The first to burst its buds is the best-known and most widely-planted of them all, the yellow-flowered *Saxifraga* × *apiculata*. This is also one of the easiest-growing and will eventually spread into a low mat up to 30 cm (12 in) across. Equally easy is *S.* 'Elizabethae', another strong grower which smothers itself with primrose-yellow flowers.

Most of the other kabschia saxifrages are still more compact than these two popular favourites, forming very tightly-packed mats or cushions of green, grey-green or silvery-grey foliage just 2.5–5 cm (1–2 in) high and about 15 cm (6 in) across. They look especially good planted where they can spread along crevices between rocks. All produce pretty little button flowers studding the tight foliage-like gems or held on tiny stems barely above ground level. A sample of those most widely available from rock plant nurseries would include: *S. burserana* and its varieties (white or yellow); 'Boston Spa' and 'Faldonside' (yellow); 'Cranbourne' and 'Jenkinsae' (pink).

S. oppositifolia is similar to the kabschia saxifrages but with a wider-spreading trailing habit that makes it a good plant for placing behind rocks to creep attractively down the rockface. The flowers sit virtually stemless on the ground-hugging foliage and may be rich purplish-red, crimson or rose-pink depending on the variety.

The alpine primulas rank alongside the kabschia saxifrages as one of the major groups of truly miniature plants for a spring display on the rock garden or raised bed. These are not the leafy border primulas, but little rosette-leaved plants which form low-growing tufts or cushions ideal for tucking in between rocks or up against the base of rockwork.

One of the loveliest and most eye-catching is *Primula marginata*, whose deeply toothed and silvery-white powdered leaves make a handsome feature even when the plants are not pushing up their short-stemmed flower heads. A number of named varieties can be found in rock plant catalogues with flowers in varying shades of clear lilac-blue.

The yellow-flowered *P. auricula* (the alpine parent of the multi-coloured border auriculas) is an old favourite, and 'Blairside Yellow' is a very dwarf variety well worth looking out for. Other good, free-flowering and easy-growing, choices include the *P.* × *pubescens* hybrids raised from *P. auricula*. These come in a range of flower colours from pink and red, through mauve and violet, to cream and white.

Better known than these is the popular 'drumstick primula', *P. denticulata*.

Although often suggested for rock gardens, this is really more of a small border plant. However, on a large rock garden or raised bed it will provide a very long-lasting display with its bold ball-shaped flower heads of lavender-blue, purple, red or white, according to the variety you choose.

The ferny-leaved 'pasque flower', *Pulsatilla vulgaris*, is another well-known and much-loved early spring rock plant, valued by gardeners for its large and showy goblet-shaped flowers, endearingly covered with fine silky hairs when in bud. The flower colour is usually violet-purple, but reddish forms are available for variety. Specialist alpine nurseries often list other, higher-alpine pulsatilla species with glistening white cup-flowers. These are still more lovely but, unfortunately, not so easy to grow.

■ *Late spring flowers*

For colour in late spring there are a number of dainty little treasures, not least of which is the stunning spring gentian, *Gentiana verna*. This is one that no miniature garden should be without: a real eye-catcher when its star-shaped flowers, of the purest sky-blue, open on 5–8 cm (2–3 in) stems above the close-knit mat of tiny leaves. The best form, with large flowers of a particularly bright clear blue, is *G. verna* 'Angulosa'. The large blue trumpets of *G. acaulis* are equally spectacular but, unfortunately, are seldom produced as freely as the starry flowers of the spring gentian.

A perfect companion plant to the gentians is the pink-flowered *Armeria caespitosa*. This is a much neater alpine version of the popular summer-flowering 'sea thrift', *A. maritima*, which is often used to good effect on larger rock gardens and raised beds. But *A. caespitosa* is the one to choose for smaller mini-gardens; and look out especially for the form 'Bevan's Variety', which is a deeper rose-pink than the ordinary type.

For an even more striking splash of pink in late spring, there is *Aethionema* 'Warley Rose'. This shrubby little plant flowers over a long period, and its mound of bluish-grey foliage is pretty to see at any time.

Ramonda myconi is a choice rosette-forming plant for a humus-enriched north slope of the rock garden or (better still) for planting in a shady wall crevice. On the rock garden, too, it is best wedged into a vertical gap between rocks facing away from the sun. In these positions the handsome, dark green, crinkly-leaved rosettes are shown off to their best advantage; and they will appreciate the shelter of the wall or rockwork against heavy winter rain (which can cause the plant's crown to rot if water collects in the rosettes, as tends to happen if it is grown on the flat). The saucer-shaped flowers are clear lavender-blue.

Where a quick mass of bright colour is required, the alpine phloxes play much the same role in late spring and early summer as the aubrietas do earlier in the season; easy-going mat plants which smother themselves with gaily-coloured flowers in a seemingly endless display.

The vigorous *Phlox subulata* varieties are suitable for larger rock gardens and raised beds, flowering in varying shades of bright pink, red, lilac-blue and pure white. For smaller gardens, choose the slightly more compact *P. douglasii* types, which come in a similar colour range. Both types make excellent fast-growing wall plants.

■ *Quick summer colour masses*

It cannot be stressed too often that you should be wary of including too many

The eye-catching silvery-cobwebbed rosettes and rose-red flower spikes of Sempervivum arachnoideum.

of the most popular fast-spreaders and mass-colour plants where the rock garden or raised bed is on the small side, and this applies as much to the summer-flowering plants as to the aubrietas and alyssums of spring. The helianthemums are typical examples, already discussed under 'Shrubs'. But as many gardeners (understandably) think of these low spreaders as rock plants rather than shrubs, they warrant another quick mention here; along with a few other space-hungry summer-flowering plants to be cautious about.

The helianthemums do provide never-ending colour all summer long, in shades of red, pink, orange, yellow and of course white. And where there is space for them to spread – to 60 cm (2 ft) or more across – then they can be extremely useful. But in smaller mini-gardens they should be treated with great caution. They look good, and prove less of a problem, where they are planted to trail down the wall of a raised bed or over rocks rather than taking up valuable growing space.

Be wary also of the popular pink-flowered carpeting plant *Saponaria ocymoides*. This one not only spreads widely but also self-seeds freely. It, too, is best trailing down a wall or over rocks where a bold summer-long colour mass is desired. It should be used with caution in the smaller rock garden.

Flowering thymes can cause problems in a small space, quickly making wide mats. In a small garden they are better avoided; or search alpine catalogues for compact varieties like *Thymus serpyllum* 'Minor'. However, all are excellent for planting in paving. Many sedums are fast spreaders which need careful consideration where space is at a premium, and the ground-covering acaenas can be a real menace. These also make good paving plants.

Avoid like the plague the rampant-growing bellflower *Campanula poscharskyana*, which can easily spread to 90 cm (3 ft) or more across by underground shoots which are the devil to weed out of a miniature garden without disturbing other plants. *C. portenschlagiana* is a popular spreading bellflower which, although not as rampant as *poscharskyana*, can prove a nuisance in small miniature gardens; so watch out for this one, too. An excellent fast-growing wall plant, however.

■ *Neat plants for summer display*

Most alpine plant nurseries can offer a wide range of far neater and less invasive campanulas, with bell flowers of blue, purple or white, to grace the rock garden or raised bed in summer; and, indeed, they are one of the major groups of rock plants for this season. There are far too many choices to list here, but the following are all excellent:

C. garganica, a strong-growing blue starry-flowered plant for larger gardens, very free-flowering and good for planting in walls.

C. 'Stella', similar to *garganica*.

C. carpatica, a bushy upright plant with large blue, purple or white upward-facing saucer-flowers.

C. cochlearifolia, dwarf plant with nodding blue or white bells, runs about by underground stems.

C. pulla, similar to *cochlearifolia*, but purple-flowered and not so strong-growing, so suited to the smallest gardens.

The alpine dianthus are generally compact mat or cushion plants which will never become a problem even in the most restricted spaces. A notable exception however, is *Dianthus deltoides*, the lovely 'maiden pink', flowering in various shades of red, pink or white. This is widely available from garden centres and is a stunning plant for larger rock gardens and raised beds, for wall gardens and planting in paving; easy-growing and very free-flowering over a long period. But it does spread quite widely and is also very free-seeding; so not a particularly good bet for small mini-gardens, where its prolific self-sown seedlings may easily become a nuisance.

If your planting space is strictly limited, choose neater species and varieties which will not seed around, such as: *D. alpinus*, green mats and large rose-pink flowers; 'La Bourbrille', very low-growing and handsome blue-grey mats and fringed scented pink blooms; or 'Whitehills', with tight cushions of tiny grey foliage and masses of small pale-pink flowers.

Another major group of refined summer-flowering alpines are the so-called 'encrusted' rosette-forming saxifrages. These take their name from the attractive silvery-grey crusty coating on the strap-shaped leaves of many of the species and varieties. This is composed of lime taken up from the soil by the plants' roots and secreted through the leaf pores, so that the rosettes are actually encrusted with a rock-like layer or stippling. Added to the charming symmetry of their perfectly-formed rosettes, this makes the encrusted saxifrages superb foliage plants that are a pleasure to see even when not in bloom. They are also some of the very best choices for planting in rock crevices and walls, where their rosettes will form impressive clumps and their long flower-plumes will cascade outwards and downwards in a stunning waterfall effect.

One of the very showiest is *Saxifraga lingulata*, with large iron-grey rosettes, silver-beaded around the leaf edges. The flower plume, packed with small blooms, may be over 30 cm (1 ft) long, so this is best in a high crevice in rockwork or a wall, where it has room to spill out and down to best effect. Another impressive species needing a similar situation is *S. cotyledon*, whose large rosettes of silver-grey edged leaves produce even larger flower plumes, up to 60 cm (2 ft) long. The most commonly available variety is the very handsome and easy-growing 'Southside Seedling', its white flowers heavily spotted with bright red.

Much neater types are also available, forming low hummocks of small silvery rosettes with far shorter flower plumes and suitable for the very smallest of miniature gardens. These include: *S. aizoon baldensis*, one of the very tiniest; *S. a. lutea*, larger, with lemon-yellow flowers; *S. a. rosea*, similar but with pink plumes; *S. cochlearis*, very silvery rosettes and white flowers; and *S. c. minor*, another real miniature.

■ Colourful foliage

The sedums and sempervivums are popular succulent-leaved carpeting plants for colourful and interesting foliage effects, plus summer flowers. But bear in mind the earlier warning that many of the faster-spreading sedums can quickly pose problems in a restricted space.

Sedum spathulifolium is one of the best of the 'stonecrops' forming low mats of fleshy grey-green leaves flushed red and purple. *S. s.* 'Purpureum' is particularly rich in its purple foliage tint, and *S. s.* 'Cappa Blanca' is completely grey-leaved with an overlying grey-white sheen that is very lovely. The flattened flower heads are bright yellow and long-lasting.

The most popular of the rosette-forming 'houseleeks' is *Sempervivum tectorum*, its large green rosettes strikingly tipped or flushed with purple-red in varying degrees according to the variety; plus tall-stemmed heads of rose-purple flowers. Rather neater growing, for the smaller rock garden or raised bed, is the fascinating *S. arachnoideum*, whose red-flushed leaves are woven together at the tips with a dense cobweb of fine white threads across the top of the compact rosettes. *S. a. laggeri* is a form with a particularly dense and attractive cobweb effect. Both produce bright rose-red flower heads.

■ Bright gentian-blues

For a splash of intense gentian-blue in the summer mini-garden there are two superb trailing plants to choose. But be warned, one of them must have lime-free soil.

The first is, of course, a gentian; the trumpet-flowered *Gentiana septemfida*. This is a little like the gorgeous autumn gentians (about which, more shortly) in sending out trailing flowering stems from a central leaf tuft, each stem bearing at its tip an upward-facing cluster of rich blue trumpets. While the autumn gentians must have lime-free conditions, this one does not mind limy soil in the least.

The second is *Lithospermum diffusum*, a low mat-forming shrubby plant which produces a non-stop succession of deep gentian-blue flowers throughout the summer months and well into autumn. This one must have lime-free soil, or a non-limy peat-based planting mixture. 'Heavenly Blue' is the most richly-coloured variety and the one most commonly available.

■ *Non-stop summer/autumn flowers*
Finally, a few more very long-flowering rock plants which will provide colour all summer long, and into autumn in some cases:

Viola cornuta is a charming little easy-growing mat-forming violet which starts its display of elegant lavender blooms in early summer and continues, on and off, into autumn. *V. c.* 'Alba' is an even lovelier pure-white version which, if anything, seems to flower still longer than the ordinary type. *V. c.* 'Minor' is a neater-growing form, ideal for smaller rock gardens and raised beds.

The low-spreading 'evening primrose' *Oenothera missouriensis* also produces its 8 cm (3 in) wide lemon-yellow flowers from early summer into autumn. Unfortunately its trailing ground-hugging stems can cover a fair area, so this is not really one for the small miniature garden.

Silene schafta forms a compact tuft of soft hairy leaves with sprays of bright pink flowers, again from the start of summer until well into the misty days of autumn. It is also very easy-growing.

Orange-red is a fairly uncommon colour amongst rock plants, and this makes the orange-hued tubular flowers of *Penstemon pinifolius* particularly eye-catching during its long summer season. This is a shrubby little plant with handsome feathery foliage made up of thin needle-shaped leaves.

Hypericum olympicum has already been described under 'Shrubs' as a good choice for summer-long colour. As it is a favourite of mine, and since many gardeners think of it more as a rock plant than a dwarf shrub, it deserves a second mention here. The freely-produced large golden saucers really are a delight for weeks on end. If you keep it compact by trimming back after flowering, it is quite suitable for small rock gardens or beds. The variety *H. o.* 'Citrinum' is equally lovely, with lemon-yellow flowers. I would not be without either of them.

Last, but by no means least, the dwarf alpine geraniums are, just like their larger border-plant cousins, classic plants for long-lasting summer-flowering displays.

First, beware of planting the magenta-crimson-flowered *Geranium sanguineum* in a miniature garden. It is a rampant grower which will climb through and over other plants. Instead, choose the neater form sold by alpine nurseries as 'Lancastriense'. This forms low mats spangled with inch-wide flowers of a clear pink hue.

Other excellent choices include:
G. cinereum, silvery foliage and light purple-pink flowers veined with darker pink or red; generally available in the variety 'Ballerina', which is particularly free-flowering.

G. subcaulescens, vivid crimson flowers with purple-black centres; a paler rose-pink in the variety 'Splendens'.

G. dalmaticum, glossy lobed leaves that take on tints of red and orange in autumn, with a long succession of pink flowers.

Opposite: Oenothera missouriensis *produces its large yellow flowers continuously throughout summer and into autumn.*

G. farreri (syn. *G. napuligerum*), a really dainty beauty with very elegant pale rose flowers.

All of these will flower throughout summer and may well carry on producing the odd bloom or two through autumn as well. Trimming back the flowering shoots as the display fades in late summer may encourage the production of an extra late-season flush of colour. And regular dead-heading, to prevent energy being wasted on seed production, will help to ensure a prolonged show.

■ *Autumn and winter*

These are difficult seasons for rock gardens and raised beds, since the number of truly miniature plants and shrubs which flower during this period are very few indeed. The answer is, of course, to boost the display with a selection of dwarf autumn-flowering and winter-flowering bulbs, corms and tubers, and these will be discussed (along with bulbs for spring and summer) in the final section of this chapter.

AUTUMN FLOWERS As I have said, some of the long-flowering summer rock plants may continue their display into autumn, but this often depends to a large degree on the weather and how advanced or retarded the seasons are compared with a normal year. If the weather turns dry or cold (or, worse still, both) then the expected late flowers may fail to appear, or be produced only sparsely. Most reliable are *Geranium cinereum*, *G. subcalescens*, *Lithospermum diffusum*, *Viola cornuta* and *Silene schafta*.

One extremely useful true autumn-flowering rock plant is *Polygonum vacciniifolium*. This is a popular and easy-growing shrubby plant which quickly spreads to form a dense ground-hugging mat of glossy evergreen leaves, smothered during autumn with short erect spikes of pale rose-red flowers. It looks especially good trailing over rockwork or down a wall. Unfortunately, it is rather vigorous for a very small rock garden or bed but is so useful for late colour that it is still worth considering; just take care to site it where it will not cause too many problems.

No such problem arises with the autumn-flowering gentians. If only these stunning beauties *would* spread so far and so fast that they became a nuisance – what a wonderful nuisance they would be! Their large trumpet-flowers, in various brilliant shades of blue, are one of the glories of the gardening year.

All form small tufts from which trailing flower shoots spread slowly outwards as autumn approaches, each one ending in an upturned trumpet or two. Lucky indeed is the gardener who finds that his soil and climate suits them so well that they make wide-spreading mats; unfortunately they are highly unlikely to pose any problems even in the smallest of rock gardens or raised beds.

Lime-free soil, or a non-limy peat-based planting mixture, is absolutely essential, otherwise these little marvels will quickly curl up and die. They also hate being dry at the roots during summer yet must have well-drained conditions to ensure that they do not rot-off in winter. If your garden soil is not limy, then they can be planted in the general soil-and-chippings mixture you should have prepared for your rock garden or raised bed, but work in plenty of peat (to retain summer moisture) and do make sure that the mixture is free-draining (add extra grit or chippings if necessary).

Where the soil is limy, plant in specially-prepared large pockets of a free-draining mixture made up with lime-free, 'ericaceous' peat compost and non-limy grit or chippings. Choose a site on a slope of the rock garden facing away from the sun. And, whether on the rock garden or raised bed, some shade from rocks, conifers, shrubs or other tall plants will be greatly appreciated.

The strongest and easiest growing types include:

Gentiana sino-ornata, one of the very finest, with deep royal-blue trumpets very freely produced.

G. × macaulayi 'Kingfisher', a vigorous grower, with similar flowers to *sino-ornata* but earlier in the season. *G. × m.* 'Kidbrooke Seedling', another strong-growing form of *× macaulayi* with rich blue flowers.

G. 'Stevenagensis', large trumpets of deepest blue.

COLOUR IN WINTER   The kabschia saxifrages discussed earlier as rock plants for early spring do, as mentioned there, start their flowering display before winter is out, so are really winter/spring plants. This is especially true of the very early-flowering *Saxifraga × apiculata*.

But the main stand-by for winter colour on rock gardens and raised beds is the wide selection of winter-spring flowering heathers, the neat-growing and lime-tolerant *Erica herbacea* (syn. *E. carnea*) varieties mentioned earlier as dwarf shrubs. Amongst the earliest-flowering of these, sometimes showing colour as early as Christmas, are 'Springwood Pink', 'Springwood White' and the old variety 'King George'.

On a large rock garden or raised bed, the 'Christmas rose', *Helleborus niger*, may be planted for its large white bowl-shaped flowers, which appear from late December onwards. But this is really a small border plant and not neat-growing enough for smaller miniature gardens. Indeed, miniature gardens rely very heavily on dwarf bulbs for winter colour, so let us now move on to these.

□ Dwarf bulbs, corms and tubers □

The usefulness of bulbs for squeezing extra seasonal colour into rock gardens and raised beds has already been referred to under 'Planting design' in Chapter 2. Remember, in particular, the benefits of underplanting trailing rock plants with bulbs to spear up through their foliage mats, making double use of the available growing space. Bear in mind also that, although the most commonly grown dwarf bulbs are the winter-flowering and spring-flowering types, those which bloom in autumn are equally desirable for additional colour in that quiet season.

The most important thing when choosing bulbs for rock gardens and raised beds (and any other type of miniature garden) is to keep them in scale with the other plants, shrubs and trees. Nothing will look more wrong than a clump of tall-stemmed and large-flowered bulbs towering above a dwarf conifer or a tiny ground-hugging alpine plant. Apart from looking out of scale, taller-growing bulbs also tend to have large leaves, which can cause real problems when they flop over onto miniature plants and smother them.

Be warned that not all of those described in catalogues as dwarf or 'rockery' bulbs are true miniatures suitable for the smallest of mini-gardens. Many are actually quite tall when put alongside the neatest dwarf conifers and rock plants, and so are only really suited to large rock gardens and raised beds, or as small bulbs for ordinary beds and borders.

All those suggested here are dainty enough for small rock gardens and beds, and many are equally suitable for miniature gardens in containers (troughs, sinks, window boxes etc) where planting space is very restricted.

■ *Winter*

The hardy cyclamen are invaluable tuberous-rooted plants for colour in autumn, winter and spring. The one to choose for a winter display is *Cyclamen coum*, whose dumpy little pink or carmine-red flowers appear before Christmas in some years and always soon after the New Year. The leaves are also handsome during winter, generally having attractive silvery markings (although some forms have plainer glossy foliage). All hardy cyclamen enjoy the well-drained conditions on a rock garden or raised bed, but they prefer to have an extra dose of peat, or other humus material, worked into their planting site.

Early-flowering crocus species are also good, and you will find a number of these listed in the catalogues of specialist dwarf bulb nurseries. *Crocus laevigatus* is the earliest of all, often starting to flower well before Christmas. The purple-veined lavender flowers are deliciously honey-scented and lovely to pick and bring indoors. This is closely followed by *C. ancyrensis* (alias 'Golden Bunch'), with small but rich yellow flowers. Other good winter-flowering choices are: *C. imperati*, with large flowers, buff with purple streaks outside annd violet-purple inside; *C. flavus* (also sold as *C. aureus*), very bright orange-yellow; and *C. sieberi*, lilac-blue.

Snowdrops are, of course, excellent bulbs for late winter and early spring flowers. The common snowdrop, *Galanthus nivalis*, is rather fast-spreading for small miniature gardens but may find a place on the larger rock garden or raised bed. Here you can also try the large-flowered Turkish snowdrop, *G. elwesii*. An excellent companion plant to these is *Eranthis hyemalis*, the 'winter aconite', which produces its bright yellow buttercup flowers around the same time. Both this and the snowdrops are like the cyclamen in enjoying plenty of moisture-retentive humus in their planting site.

The dwarf bulbous reticulata irises are superb for early colour and revel in the same extra well-drained soil conditions as alpine plants. Earliest of all, flowering in the heart of winter, are the very dwarf canary-yellow-flowered *Iris danfordiae* and the brilliant sky-blue *I. histrioides* 'Major'. These are closely followed by the many colour forms and varieties of *I. reticulata* (from which this group of bulbs take their name) flowering in shades of blue, purple-blue and purple-red.

Narcissus asturiensis is the very tiniest daffodil species at just 8 cm (3 in) tall and will produce its diminutive yellow trumpets from mid-winter onwards.

Lastly, to carry the display on from late winter to spring there are the blue, pink, magenta-red and white varieties of *Anemone blanda*.

■ *Early spring*

The miniature crocus species and their varieties are the major contributors to the spring bulb display on rock gardens and raised beds, especially the many colour forms of the popular and easy-growing *Crocus chrysanthus*.

These come in various shades of blue and yellow, plus cream and white, and they give marvellous value for growing space, each corm producing a large number of flowers one after another over a long period in late winter and early spring. The best varieties include 'Blue Pearl'; 'Cream Beauty'; 'E.A. Bowles' (rich yellow); 'Snow Bunting' (white); 'Zwanenberg Bronze' (yellow and bronze); and 'Ladykiller' and 'Eyecatcher' (both white and purple-blue).

The following are all equally reliable miniature species and varieties: *C. biflorus* 'Alexandri' (white and purple); *C. minimus* (one of the very tiniest, ideal for miniature trough gardens); *C. sieberi* 'Violet Queen' (violet-blue); and *C. susianus* (rich orange-yellow).

Chionodoxas are wonderful little bulbs, forming pools of vivid blue in the early spring garden. The smallest is *Chionodoxa sardensis*, with star flowers of deep gentian-blue. *C. luciliae* is taller and stronger with dainty spikes of white-centred blue flowers. And *C. gigantea* has especially large but less intensely-coloured flowers.

The dwarf scillas are also good for a splash of blue. *Scilla bifolia* (masses of starry little blue flowers) and *S. tubergeniana* (pale silvery-blue flowers, striped darker blue) are both the neatest growers and the earliest-flowering species.

Narcissus bulbocodium and its varieties are enchanting with their early-season golden 'hoop-petticoat' shaped trumpets. And equally charming is *N. cyclamineus*, a dwarf species trumpet daffodil with unusual swept-back cyclamen-like petals. While the 'hoop-petticoat' types enjoy general well-drained rock garden and raised bed conditions, *cyclamineus* prefers plenty of peat in the soil.

■ *Late spring*

For late spring colour, there are the dwarf tulip species. Many of the hybrid dwarf varieties listed by bulb firms as 'rockery tulips' are actually rather tall

The yellow crocus-like flowers of the sternbergias are useful for a bright autumn display.

and/or large-flowered to look right in smaller miniature gardens. But the following are some of the very neatest small-flowered types: *Tulipa batalinii* (delicate primrose-yellow flowers); *T. maximowiczii* (similar, but vivid scarlet); *T. tarda* (masses of wide-open creamy-white flowers with a yellow centre); and *T. urumiensis* (golden-yellow, bronze on the outside).

Also flowering in late spring is the pretty ivy-leaved and rose-pink flowered *Cyclamen repandum*. Like the winter-flowering *C. coum*, this enjoys plenty of humus (peat, etc.) in its planting site.

■ *Summer*

The vast majority of summer-flowering bulbs are far too tall-growing for rock gardens and raised beds (or most other types of miniature garden). However, the following are excellent choices:

Oxalis adenophylla forms a neat clump of attractively crinkled clover-like greyish leaves, spangled with satin-pink cup-shaped flowers in late spring and early summer.

Cyclamen europaeum (now more correctly *C. purpurascens*), produces its carmine-red scented flowers from late summer to early autumn, above handsome silver-marbled leaves.

Rhodohypoxis baurii forms tufts of hairy narrow leaves covered throughout the summer months with rose-red, pink or white star-shaped flowers.

The summer-flowering alliums are popular bulbs, but most are much too large and fast-spreading for the average rock garden or raised bed. Here are some of the real miniatures, all free-flowering and quite lovely: *Allium beesianum* (bright blue); *A. cyaneum* (eye-catching cobalt-blue); *A. flavum* 'Minus' (yellow); and *A. narcissiflorum* (dangling rose-purple bells, one of the loveliest).

■ *Autumn*

Hardy cyclamen play an especially valuable role at this time of year, providing masses of freely-produced dainty pink and white flowers over a long period.

Best-known is *Cyclamen neapolitanum* (now more correctly *C. hederifolium*) whose bright pink flowers spring leafless from the bare earth, to be shortly followed by a very handsome carpet of ivy-like green leaves strikingly marked with silver. These provide an attractive feature throughout winter after the flowers are over. The pure white-flowered *C. n.* 'Album' is, if anything, still more enchanting and a mixed planting of this and the pink type looks particularly charming. *C. cilicium* is especially dainty, with delicate shell-pink flowers and silver-marbled rounded leaves.

Equally desirable for this season are the autumn-flowering crocus. Most widely available is the lilac-pink flowered *Crocus zonatus* (alias *kotschyanus*) but the form sold in most shops and garden centres tends to be very shy-flowering. Take care to buy from a specialist miniature bulb nursery which guarantees a free-flowering form.

The following are all superb autumn crocus species, less well-known than *C. zonatus* but well worth seeking out in bulb catalogues: *C. goulimyi* (lilac flowers); *C. medius* (rich lilac-purple); *C. nudiflorus* (deep violet-purple); and *C. speciosus* (various colour forms available, from pale lavender-blue to deep violet-blue, plus a stunning pure white form).

And, finally, *Sternbergia lutea* will add a touch of bright yellow to the autumn miniature garden with its crocus-like flowers.

CHAPTER FOUR

PLANTING IN PAVING

Anumber of the tougher and lower-growing rock plants will thrive in gaps and crevices between paving slabs, transforming paths, patios and other bare utilitarian areas into attractive features.

Gravelled paths and areas, too, may be planted with resilient low-spreading plants which will not object too much to being trodden on from time to time.

In either case, there are two vital points to bear in mind: (a) that the majority of the plants should be types which form very low ground-hugging mats or cushions that are easily stepped over and will not become a serious inconvenience to the normal use of the path or area, and (b) that the soil beneath the paving crevices or patches of gravel to be planted should be well prepared, just as it would be for plants in rock gardens, raised beds or any other miniature-garden situation.

□ Soil improvement and planting □

The basic soil-improvement advice given for rock gardens (removing all weed roots, adding grit or chippings for drainage, plus peat or other humus material to retain summer moisture) should be followed here. Take care to prepare the ground thoroughly. Dig out the top-soil, break up the sub-soil in the base of the hole, and refill with the improved top-soil mixture. Make sure, also, that you do not just prepare a narrow pocket of soil immediately below the paving crevice or little patch of gravel where the plant is to go. Ensure that the area of improved soil is wide enough so that the plant can spread its roots freely beneath the surrounding slabs or gravel, for a cool and moist summer root-run.

This is most easily done at the time of laying the paving or gravel. With existing gravelled areas it is, of course, only a matter of scraping away the chippings and getting to work. Where existing paving is concerned, you will have to break corners off slabs here and there (using a heavy hammer) to create planting holes if no gaps large enough for easy planting are already available. Gaps of about 15 cm (6 in) across will allow you to get a trowel in, to remove, improve and replace the soil below the hole and a few inches around, beneath the surrounding paving.

If the paving has been cemented in place, then you will have no option but to work in this way. But if it proves possible to lift, break and re-set slabs which were previously laid dry, then making planting crevices and soil preparation will be that much easier.

Above: *Choose mainly low-spreading plants, which will not prove too much of an obstacle, for planting in paving.*

Opposite: *Bushier plants may be placed towards the edges of paths and paved areas, where they will not get in the way too much.*

When laying new paving, you will similarly need to break the corners from rectangular or square slabs, before setting them in place, to provide suitable planting holes a few inches wide. And, naturally, here you can do the soil improvement and planting as you go along. Planting in the gaps after construction is perfectly feasible (provided the crevices are large enough) but it is easier to plant correctly and snugly during laying. If you are putting down 'crazy' paving made up of broken slabs or stones, then arranging planting gaps is, of course, no problem at all.

■ Planting methods

As for the actual planting, the advice given under 'Planting and maintenance' for rock gardens and raised beds should be followed here as well. In particular, remember to top-dress the soil in the planting crevices with a layer of stone chippings, taking care to spread these under the foliage and around the necks of the plants (Fig. 8). This will provide an attractive finish, and prevent unsightly soil-splashing during heavy rain, while the plants fill the gaps between the paving. It will also, as on rock gardens and raised beds, help to prevent weeds seeding into the crevices and keep the necks of the plants dry during wet winter weather, when they are most prone to rotting-off if waterlogged.

Be sure to water the plants in very thoroughly, and keep them watered during dry spells in spring and summer until well established. As for feeding, applying solid fertilizer is obviously a problem; instead, two or three doses during spring and summer of a high-potash liquid feed (liquid tomato fertilizer will do) should keep the plants growing and flowering well.

In addition to planting in large gaps, narrow cracks between existing or newly-laid slabs may be seeded with suitable plants by mixing the seed with sand and sprinkling this into the crevices. Take care to keep the cracks well watered in dry weather to aid germination and help the seedlings establish. Suggestions for suitable seed choices are given later.

Finally, do remember that paving should be firmly bedded on sand (or even more solid foundations) to ensure stability. If you are going to be doing a lot of planting between the slabs or stones, then a sand-bedding layer is a particularly good idea, as the small plants will enjoy rooting into this as well as into the pockets of prepared soil. Do not forget, either, that patios and paths adjoining walls (either house walls or garden walls) should be laid with a very slight

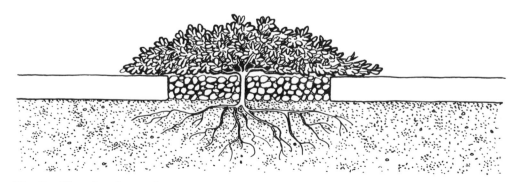

Fig. 8 Planting in paving
Prepare a wide pocket of improved soil beneath the paving planting hole (adding peat and grit or chippings) to encourage the plants to quickly spread their roots under the slabs. Top-dress around the necks of the plants with stone chippings.

slope so that rainwater run-off will drain away from the wall and not collect in puddles. This is especially important where the paving is to be planted, otherwise there is a danger of plants becoming waterlogged where rain collects.

□ Planting design □

As I have said, the majority of plants in paved or gravelled areas should be as low-growing as possible, for obvious practical reasons. However, a little variety in height and scale will greatly enhance what is, after all, going to be just as much a feature to be admired as it is a place to walk or sit-out during summer.

The occasional bushier plant should not pose too much of an obstacle even on a path; especially if it is a garden-walk path, used mainly for strolling through the garden rather than for heavy daily use; and particularly if the bushier plants are kept to the sides of the path, with only very low mat-forming plants in the centre.

In a larger area of gravel or paving, such as a patio, there is even more scope for introducing variety of height and scale in the plantings. Here it is still easier (given the extra space available) to site one or two bushier and taller plants towards the edges, where they will not get in the way too much. Indeed, there may even be room to plant the odd dwarf conifer or miniature shrub (making sure, of course, that they are very slow-growing types, and that they are offset to one side, where they will not be too much of a nuisance). This will complete the picture and create a veritable garden-in-miniature effect.

Another alternative is to leave (or make) a large enough planting space somewhere in the paved or gravelled area to allow you to plant a small group of, for example, a very slow-growing conifer, a bushy rock plant, and one or two trailers or mat-forming plants. This may act as a focal-point, with other plants scattered in the surrounding paving or gravel, or it may stand alone as a miniature garden in its own right.

The general garden-planting design rules apply as much here as in any miniature-gardening situation: aim for a mix of plants to provide colour and interest in different seasons, and plan contrasts in height (within the obvious limitations), growth habit and foliage between neighbouring plants.

□ Choosing the plants □

As always, the golden rule is to make sure that you choose plants to suit the available space and the situation. In a large paved or gravelled area it may be possible (or even desirable) to include some very vigorous and fast-spreading plants for quick effect; ground-covering prostrate conifers, helianthemums, aubrietas and suchlike. But the less room you have to play with, the more care you should take to choose neater plants which will not grow too tall nor spread too far. Naturally, this is particularly vital in paving and gravel, where over-vigorous plants may not just overwhelm smaller neighbouring plants if space is strictly limited, but may also cause serious obstructions.

At the smallest end of the scale, you may be planting a little stone-paved or gravel path laid specifically to border a rock garden or raised bed (or to run through the middle of a large rock garden). In this situation, you may even treat the path as an extension of the rock garden or raised bed; improving the

A selection of bulbs for different seasons makes for an unusual and interesting feature in a large planting gap in paving; seen here, showy autumn-flowering colchicums.

soil more generally (with chippings and peat) before laying the paving or gravel, and including a few choicer and daintier alpines amongst the more resilient and trample-resistant plants. If the path is not intended for heavy use, but mainly as a place from which to admire and weed the rock garden or bed, then these little treasures should come to no harm and, on the contrary, will provide a lovely complementary feature.

Indeed, rock plant enthusiasts sometimes deliberately construct small 'alpine pavement' gardens in this way, as an adjunct to the main rock garden; bedding flat rocks into a level patch of thoroughly improved soil, exactly as for the rock garden. Here, even the choicest alpines recommended in the previous chapter for rock gardens and raised beds, may safely be grown, protected from excess winter wet by well-drained soil below and rain-shielding stones above.

The flat stones should, incidentally, be tilted very slightly away from the centre of the pavement, to carry away rainwater during winter downpours. Such alpine pavements are, of course, not meant to be frequently and heavily used as pathways, since this would compact the soil mixture beneath the stones, spoiling the well-drained conditions that the alpines depend on.

■ *Low-spreading plants*
The following are all low-growing trailers, mat-forming or cushion plants suitable for planting in paving or gravel.

>*Note*: Where a plant name is marked by an asterisk * and little or no description is given, refer to Chapter 3 for further information.

As I mentioned in the previous chapter, the mat-forming thymes are too vigorous for most rock gardens and raised beds. However, they are extremely popular choices for paving and gravel, being tough and trample-resistant, and highly aromatic when stepped on. The best of the low-growing types are the summer-flowering *Thymus serpyllum* varieties: 'Annie Hall' (pale pink flowers); 'Pink Chintz' (rich rose-pink); 'Coccineus' (deep red); and 'Albus' (white-flowered).

Nierembergia repens (also sometimes sold as *N. rivularis*) is another firm favourite with large and almost stemless upward-facing white cup-shaped flowers; again, summer-flowering.

Also good is the easy-growing and very low-carpeting *Acaena microphylla*. The bronze-green foliage is handsome at all times, covered during summer with spiny crimson seed-heads.

The mat-forming sedums and the rosette-leaved spreading sempervivums are commonly grown in paving and gravel for their handsome foliage tints and summer flowers. The best choices include the *Sedum spathulifolium** varieties, *Sempervivum arachoideum laggeri** and the various foliage-colour forms of *S. tectorum**.

For masses of bright colour over a long period in late spring the alpine phloxes* are excellent low-trailing plants, quite at home in paving and looking particularly good planted in gravel. One of my personal favourites is the very easy-growing and free-seeding *Dianthus deltoides**. Once established, this will quickly seed itself into the tiniest of cracks and crevices (or in surrounding gravel). And *Campanula portenshlagiana** will run swiftly along crevices between paving slabs, again working its way into the tiniest cracks, by means of underground runners; not such a good idea for gravel, though, unless there is plenty of room for its mats to spread far and wide.

Rather daintier mat-forming and cushion rock plants for small paved or gravelled areas include: *Armeria caespitosa**, *Dianthus alpinus**, *D.* 'La Bourbrille'*, *Gentiana acaulis**, *Saxifraga* × *apiculata** and *S.* 'Elizabethae'*. And *Campanula cochlearifolia** is a very dinky little bellflower which will run cheerfully around in paving or gravel.

Between them, this selection of less invasive little plants will provide flowers for late winter, spring and summer; which shows what you can do with a few small plants even in a tiny area.

■ Bushy plants

Where there is space for one or two bushier plants, to add variety to a paving or gravel mini-garden, choose those which do not spread sideways excessively. And, naturally, they should be of a height that you can step over, if necessary, without too much difficulty (20–25 cm (8–10 in) or less) although, of course, these taller plants should be sited towards the edges of the paving of gravel, where they will not prove so much of an obstacle.

My first choice would always be that shrubby little yellow-flowered beauty *Hypericum olympicum**, for neat growth and summer-long colour. *Campanula carpatica** is another one for a prolonged summer display. And for winter and spring, the *Erica herbacea* (syn. *E. carnea*)* varieties are compact little heathers which look good and grow perfectly well in paving or gravel if given plenty of humus (peat, etc.) in the planting soil, to keep their roots moist in summer. And for a really special low-growing shrubby plant, you could not choose better than the highly fragrant-flowered *Daphne cneorum**.

Dwarf clump-forming ornamental grasses are also ideal for paths and other paved or gravelled areas, such as the popular tufty blue-leaved fescue, *Festuca glauca*.

■ Plants for shady areas

The plants mentioned so far are suitable for sunny paved or gravelled areas. Should you be seeking plants for paving in a shadier corner, all of the following are good.

'Mossy' saxifrages are very popular and easy-growing hummocky mat-forming plants for shade. Their moss-like foliage is attractive all year, and smothered with red, pink or white flowers in spring. 'Cloth of Gold' is a specially low-growing variety with bright golden foliage and white flowers, extremely useful for brightening-up dark corners.

Saxifraga umbrosa primuloides 'Elliott's Variety' is a diminutive 'London Pride' with sprays of rich pink summer flowers; also very easy.

Viola labradorica 'Purpurea'; a fast-spreading violet with handsome purple-tinged leaves and mauve flowers over a long period in late spring and early summer.

The well-known, wine-red flowered dwarf primrose *Primula × pruhoniciana* 'Wanda' (syn. *P. juliana* 'Wanda') will happily fill a large paving crevice in shade with its compact dark green crinkly foliage, and will provide welcome colour for months on end during late winter and spring.

A lovely ornamental grass for shady paved areas is *Millium effusum* 'Aureum', or Bowles'· golden grass; forming low clumps of bright lemon-yellow leaves, particularly colourful in spring.

And, of course, small ferns are obvious choices. One of the easiest and most handsome is the ordinary hart's tongue fern, *Asplenium scolopendrium*, whose crinkled evergreen strap-shaped fronds are a common sight growing wild in dry stone walls.

Finally, plants which may easily be established in narrow paving crevices by sowing seeds include *Campanula carpatica*, *C. cochlearifolia*, *Dianthus deltoides*, *Hypericum olympicum*, *Millium effusum* 'Aureum', thymes, and *Viola cornuta*. But, of course, seed of any low-spreading rock plants may be tried.

SMALL AND MINIATURE PLANTS FOR BORDERS AND BEDS

Over the years, many traditional and popular fast-growing shrubs and tall, space-hungry border plants have become increasingly inappropriate to the scale of small modern gardens. What a great number of today's gardeners are looking for is a range of slower-growing shrubs and more compact plants to suit their strictly limited planting areas; plants and shrubs which will not get out of hand and become a nuisance even in the tightest of spaces.

There are a great many small and miniature shrubs, plants and bulbs suitable for ordinary garden borders, and in a very small garden it is quite feasible to plant almost entirely with these; thereby packing as much variety and interest as possible into what little growing room is available. A few taller plants will always be desirable (a small tree, the odd larger shrub or loftier border plant) for variety of height and scale. But the plantings may very largely consist of neater and tinier treasures.

However, small and miniature border plants, shrubs and bulbs are, of course, not only for small gardens. Even the largest of gardens may contain some narrow borders or other tight corners, where a few neater-growing plants will prove extremely useful. And in any garden planting scheme there is a need for low-growing plants and shrubs for the fronts of borders and as edgings, and to provide a contrast to the larger elements of the border design. Then there is the sheer charm that many of these daintier plants and shrubs possess, and which attracts gardeners to them even where there is ample space to plant faster-growing and coarser items for a quicker effect.

Indeed, always going for the quickest effect, using the fastest-growing plants and shrubs available will often lead to disappointment. You will generally find that you have planted pretty much what everyone else in the area who wanted a quickly-filled garden has planted; so your borders may end up looking rather undistinguished and 'ordinary'. And fast-growing shrubs may be great for rapidly filling empty spaces, but they also tend to be some of the largest shrubs available, which may end up much taller and (more importantly) far wider-spreading than you expected.

The greatest disappointment, however, may come (especially in a small garden) when you realize that your overcrowded quick-effect plantings could have contained much greater variety and interest; if only you had taken a longer-term view and included more of the slower-growing and compact plants.

□ Planting borders and beds □

As far as planting layout is concerned, this is basically a simple matter of placing most of the taller shrubs and plants towards the back of the border or the centre of the bed, with smaller plants and shrubs in the foreground.

As mentioned previously, this is only a very basic rule which should not be followed too rigidly. You do need to contrive contrasts of height and scale here and there by placing the odd tall shrub or plant towards the fore, amongst lower-growing plants; and vice-versa. Remember that you can add further interest to the bed or border by arranging contrasts not only in height, but also in shape, growth habit, foliage colours and leaf forms (see Chapter 1, 'Making plans').

Try to ensure that the bed or border will give you colour and interest all year round, by choosing a range of plants for different seasons. In borders, this is best achieved by mixed planting of shrubs, perennial plants and bulbs. This gives you a wide choice when planning for spring, summer, autumn and winter, and it is by far the best policy for small gardens. Purely herbaceous borders, on the other hand, tend to look very bare and uninteresting during late autumn, winter and early spring. Shrub borders are easily maintained features which do not require much work once established, but they lack the variety and the prolonged and constant year-round display that a mix of shrubs, perennials and bulbs offers.

■ Foliage interest

Evergreen shrubs and plants provide foliage interest throughout the year, especially those with colourful leaf tints. But take care not to go overboard with evergreen shrubs (including conifers) in borders. The trouble with planting too many of these is that they remain unchanging, apart from their flowering display, from one season to the next. Deciduous shrubs, on the other hand, change with the season, from fresh spring growth to darker summer foliage, often handsome autumn leaf colours, and sometimes interesting or colourful bare winter branches and twigs. Aim for a·balanced mix of both types, for year-round foliage plus seasonal variety that will alter the look of the border from one part of the year to the next.

It is not just shrubs which can offer the gardener handsome evergreen

Opposite: *A good selection of easy-growing rock plants, small border perennials and dwarf shrubs, including the ferny-leaved Japanese maple* Acer palmatum *'Dissectum'* (to rear of border on right).

leaves. A number of border perennials are reliably evergreen and therefore especially valuable for year-long foliage interest as well as flowering display. Seek these out in nursery catalogues, to help clothe the bare soil when the herbaceous plants take their winter rest.

Many rock plants have attractive evergreen foliage, and this is one reason why the stronger-growing types are so useful for planting towards the front of borders or as edgings; that, and of course the fact that they are ideal low-growing 'frontal' plants. Indeed, few perennials are neater-growing than the rock plants, which makes the easier kinds especially good choices for cramming in lots of variety and flowers for different seasons in smaller borders; in combination, naturally, with small border plants, shrubs and bulbs.

■ *Bulbs for extra seasonal colour*

Dwarf bulbs, too, are just as useful here as in rock gardens and raised beds for squeezing in additional seasonal colour between the plants and shrubs. Their neater leaves generally take up less room than taller types of bulb and tend to be less of a nuisance after flowering. And, as on the rock garden or raised bed, they can be popped into gaps between plants and will not mind too much if their planting sites are eventually covered by the spreading foliage of low-growing plants.

This is a good scheme for getting double value from the available ground-space and ensuring that there are no ugly gaps in the border when spring-flowering bulbs die down for the summer. The bulbs may be used to underplant low mats of evergreen plant foliage, through which they will happily grow up. Or the bulbs may be tucked in between herbaceous plants which will spread their new season's foliage over the bulbs as they die down.

For these situations, the taller types of dwarf bulb (those which are rather too large for rock gardens, but still much neater than ordinary border bulb varieties) are the ideal choice; such things as the dwarf hybrid trumpet daffodils and tulips. These generally have enough height to their flower stems to compete with small border plants, yet are neat enough to prove great space-savers where growing room is strictly limited.

Many of the tiniest bulbs recommended earlier for rock gardens and raised beds are suitable for the very front of a border, along with the lowest-growing edging plants. They also make superb underplantings to deciduous shrubs, where they will carpet the ground in spring, before the shrubs come fully into leaf.

□ Soil preparation □

The soil preparation for small and miniature plants in garden borders obviously need not be anywhere near as thorough as for miniature plants in rock gardens and raised beds. The daintiest high-alpines which demand the extremely well drained conditions of those situations are, naturally, not suited to border planting.

Provided the soil is fairly well drained and not prone to waterlogging after heavy rain, then most of the small and miniature plants suitable for garden borders will be quite happy. However, heavy and clayey soils should be improved by the addition of coarse sand plus plenty of humus material (peat, compost, etc.) to lighten the ground and improve drainage. This is especially important where those stronger-growing rock plants which will grow happily in borders are to be sited. And it is even more essential where dwarf bulbs are going in the border – particularly the tiniest sorts, which detest badly-drained soil conditions. Incidentally, planting these little beauties beneath the branches and in the roots of shrubs will help to keep them dry during their summer rest period and ensure the kind of conditions that the majority of them enjoy.

Soil preparation for peat beds and conifer-and-heather beds (which is rather more specific to the needs of the plants to be grown) will be dealt with later in the book.

□ Rock plants for borders □

In ordinary garden borders, where the easy-growing rock plants will be amongst the smallest elements of your planting scheme, there is less need to worry about speed of growth and ultimate spread than on a rock garden or raised bed (where fast-spreading plants may very easily swamp tinier treasures). In the border there will be fewer (if any) really tiny gems that the more rampant rock plants can overrun.

Just the same, you should still tailor your plant selections to the available space, and try to avoid placing fast spreaders too close to any choicer little plants which they might eventually smother. After all, a narrow border in a small garden may offer the gardener no more growing room than the average rock garden (and quite possibly less).

In addition, where space is limited it always makes sense to aim to squeeze in a wide range of different little plants, for the variety and interest that they will provide, rather than to fill up your valuable border room with too many wide-spreading 'everyday' plants.

The following rock plants will thrive under ordinary garden border conditions provided the soil is reasonably well drained (add coarse sand and peat where the soil is heavy or clayey).

Note: Where a plant name is followed by * and little or no description is given, refer to Chapter 3 for further details.

■ *Spring*

Obvious choices for masses of border-front colour in spring are the easy-growing aubrietas* and alyssums*. But these really are edging plants for large borders only. Where space is limited, go for neater-growing plants which will not take up so much room nor require regular cutting-back after flowering to keep them compact.

The alpine phloxes are even more colourful and almost as long-flowering, but rather less invasive and much classier mat-forming plants for late spring and early summer colour. Easiest and most vigorous are the *Phlox subulata** varieties. For very small borders, choose the somewhat tidier-growing *P. douglasii** types. The phloxes, like the commoner alyssums and aubrietas, may be kept neater by trimming hard when the flowering display ends.

The above are all plants for sunny borders. For easy-growing spring colour in shadier spots, choose the crimson, pink and white flowered varieties of the 'mossy' saxifrage, *Saxifrage moschata*. And for late spring to early summer flowers in shade, *S. umbrosa primuloides* 'Elliott's Variety', a tiny pink-flowered 'London pride', is superb.

*Pulsatilla vulgaris**, the popular 'pasque flower', is a real beauty for a sunny spot in a well-drained border, its large violet-purple goblet flowers a delight in spring, and its ferny foliage pretty to see throughout summer.

The spring trumpet gentian, *Gentiana acaulis*, makes a tidy low mat for the border front. Although the large blue trumpet-flowers are not always freely produced, they are a stunning sight if this beauty does decide to put on a good display for you.

■ *Summer*

*Dianthus deltoides** and other easy rock garden 'pinks' provide handsome mats of evergreen foliage, plus a long summer flowering season. The dwarf 'rockery pink' hybrids such as 'Spencer Bickham' (deep pink flowers) and 'Pike's Pink' (double flowers) are good choices.

Thrifts are also popular for their prolonged display of pink summer flowers, and their tight grassy-leaved evergreen hummocks are ideal for edging borders. *Armeria maritima* is the well-known and widely-planted 'sea thrift' which will quickly spread to form a wide mat. For tinier borders, the alpine *A. caespitosa** is a neater-growing choice, flowering in late spring and early summer. And for a touch of rich blue in the summer border, choose the trailing *Gentiana septemfida**, the easiest of all the gentians, and not too space-hungry.

All the stronger-growing alpine bellflowers are suitable for sunny borders, where they are invaluable for providing long-lasting splashes of blue during the summer months. *Campanula carpatica** and *C. garganica** are ideal. The rather more invasive *C. portenschlagiana* is decidedly wide-spreading and only suitable for larger borders. And beware the rampant *C. poscharskyana* which should not be planted unless there is plenty of room for it to spread.

The helianthemums, too, make rather wide mats for really small borders (where two or three neater plants may be squeezed into the same space as one helianthemum) but they do offer a non-stop show of bright summer flowers where there is space to accommodate them.

Above: *Narrow borders and beds cry out for a selection of small plants and slow-growing shrubs and conifers.*

Opposite: *Conifers, rock plants, small perennials and ferns mingle in a well-planted bed.*

Other easy low-growing plants for a very long summer display (often lasting into autumn) include the yellow-flowered *Oenothera missouriensis**, *Saponaria ocymoides** (pink flowers), *Silene schafta** (bright pink), *Viola cornuta** (lavender-blue or white), and the scarlet and crimson flowered *Mimulus cupreus* varieties such as 'Whitecroft Scarlet' (ideal for shady borders). And for long-lasting autumn colour, there is of course the vigorous mat-forming and pink-flowered *Polygonum vaccinifolium**.

Sedums* and sempervivums* are useful mat-forming plants for year-round colourful foliage, plus summer flowers, in sunny borders. And a nice little carpeter for foliage effect in shade is the purple-leaved *Viola labradorica* 'Purpurea' (mauve spring flowers).

□ Small border perennials □

Few of these small perennials are much over 30 cm (1 ft) in height, and many are considerably neater than that. All are ideal for small garden borders, or for frontal positions in larger borders. Remember to check recommended planting distances in catalogues and/or reference books, to avoid overcrowding problems. And do not forget to ensure year-round interest in your borders by selecting a good mix of plants for different seasons.

■ *Spring*

For easy-growing but charming early spring flowers, there are few small perennials to beat the primroses. In local garden centres and shops you will find, at the appropriate season, various strains of highly-bred and large-flowered primroses and polyanthus, and these are excellent for masses of bright colour.

Rather more elegant and dainty are the primroses under the name *P. × pruhoniciana*. These form very compact mats and tufts of neat little crinkly leaves smothered with short-stemmed flowers from late winter to spring. Best known and most widely planted is the wine-red 'Wanda', a very easy and vigorous little primrose which blooms exceptionally freely and over a long period. Others to look out for include 'Blue Riband' (bright sky-blue), and 'Garryarde Guinevere' (leaves flushed bronze-purple, and soft pink flowers).

The wild primrose, *Primula vulgaris*, is equally valuable for its enchanting and freely-produced pale yellow winter-spring flowers; but of course it should never be taken from the countryside, so be sure to buy seed-raised plants from a nursery or garden centre. Try also the lilac–pink variety *P.v. sibthorpii*.

Primroses do not enjoy too much sun, so are especially valuable for shadier borders and gloomy corners of the garden. They also like plenty of humus in the soil.

Another classic group of winter-spring flowering small border perennials is the hellebores. Many have handsome and unusual yellowish-green flowers, but most popular are the purple-red, pink and white forms of the lenten rose, *Helleborus orientalis*. In addition to large and colourful saucer-shaped flowers, these also boast attractive hand-shaped leaves which are near-evergreen. Another popular choice is the Christmas rose, *Helleborus niger*, but this will be discussed later, as a plant for winter. All the hellebores will grow and flower well in either sun or shade, but they do prefer a shadier spot.

Also good for early flowers are: *Primula denticulata*, the easy-growing drumstick primula, with rounded flower-heads in colour ranges from lavender-blue to mauve-purple and lilac-pink to carmine-red, plus white. The sweet-scented violet, *Viola odorata*, with flowers of (most commonly) purple-blue or white. And the bright blue-flowered varieties of *Pulmonaria angustifolia*, 'Azurea' and 'Munstead Blue'.

For colour later in the spring, and for shady areas, the semi-evergreen epimediums are lovely carpeting plants. Their leaves take on various tints of pink, red, yellow and bronze as the seasons change and provide handsome ground-cover during winter. The small but elegant flowers may be red, pink, yellow or white according to the species.

Other excellent choices for late spring are the well-known London pride, *Saxifraga umbrosa* (sprays of pink flowers, good for shady borders), *Euphorbia myrsinites* (a dwarf 'spurge' with bright yellow flower bracts above blue-grey fleshy leaves); *E. epithymoides* (syn. *E. polychroma*) (sulphur-yellow flower bracts), *Iris graminea* (a dwarf lilac-purple-flowered iris, with a rich 'plummy' scent), and shooting stars, *Dodecatheon meadia* and *D. pulchellum* (red, pink or white cyclamen-like flowers; best in shade).

■ *Early summer*
Incarvillea delavayi and *I. mairei* are exotic small perennials for early summer, their large purplish-pink trumpet flowers providing an eye-catching show for weeks on end. Give them a sunny site and lots of peat in the soil.

Primula sikkimensis, the Himalayan cowslip, is one of the neatest of the border primulas (many of which can get quite large) and is a real beauty for early summer, with richly scented dangling bell-flowers of bright lemon-yellow. Give this plenty of peat in the soil as well, and preferably some shade.

Another choice plant for this time of year is *Roscoea cautleoides*, whose yellow orchid-like flowers, produced in spikes above lance-shaped leaves, are guaranteed to attract attention in any border. This is another one which likes a good dose of humus in the soil; either in sun or shade.

The border pinks are ever-popular plants for summer colour, sweet scent and handsome clumps of silver-grey foliage which will provide attractive year-round ground cover. Reliable varieties include *Dianthus* 'Diane' (double salmon-red flowers), *D.* 'Doris' (double rose-pink) and that old favourite *D.* 'Mrs. Sinkins' (double white).

Border campanulas are valuable for their blue summer flowers, but most are on the tall side. *Campanula persicifolia* is one of the most elegant, with airy spikes of blue or white bells and rosette-shaped clumps of evergreen leaves. However, where growing room is strictly limited (or just for a charming miniature effect) choose *C. lactiflora* 'Pouffe', which makes a low mound of leaves less than 30 cm (1 ft) high, set with lavender-blue bells throughout summer and into autumn.

■ *Summer-long flowers*
Geraniums are wonderful plants for prolonged summer flowering. One of the lowest-growing, and excellent for quick ground-cover, is the crimson-magenta-flowered bloody crane's-bill, *Geranium sanguineum*. Also good low mat-forming plants are *G. renardii* (handsome greyish leaves and lavender-mauve flowers), *G. endressii* 'Wargrave Pink' (clear pink flowers), *G.* 'Russell Prichard' (grey leaves and carmine red flowers) and *G. wallichianum* 'Buxton's Blue' (white-centred blue flowers).

Other long-flowering dwarf summer perennials include the large, yellow-

flowered, trailing evening primrose, *Oenothera missouriensis*, the ferny-leaved *Dicentra eximia* and *D. formosa* with their distinctive heart-shaped pink flowers (both grow and flower well in sun or shade), *Platycodon grandiflorum mariesii* (a dwarf form of the campanula-like 'balloon flower') and the yellow Welsh poppy, *Meconopsis cambrica* (be warned, though; this easy-growing little plant is a charmer for sunny or shady borders but seeds about very freely and can be a pest in small borders).

The feathery flower plumes of dwarf astilbes will provide bright colour over a long period during late summer, and sometimes into early autumn. Especially neat little varieties include *Astilbe chinensis pumila* (lilac-rose flowers above dark green ferny foliage) and *A. simplicifolia* 'Sprite' (shell pink flower sprays, followed by dark red seed heads). Give them shade, plenty of peat, and water well in dry weather for best results.

Hostas are bold-leaved foliage plants for shady borders, with lilac, mauve or white flower spikes in late summer and early autumn. Various miniature types are available, including *Hosta minor* (dark green leaves and violet flowers), *H. m.* 'Alba' (white flower spikes), *H.* 'Gold Edger' (golden-yellow foliage) and *H.* 'Ginko Craig' (green leaves, edged white).

Also good for colourful low-growing foliage in shady spots throughout summer are the variously tinted leaf forms of *Ajuga reptans*, such as 'Burgundy Glow' (green and wine-red).

Above: *Alpine geraniums make good low-growing and free-flowering plants for summer colour in borders and beds.*

Opposite: Euphorbia myrsinites *is an attractive low-spreading perennial with succulent blue-grey foliage.*

■ *Autumn and winter*

The border display may be boosted in these seasons with a range of invaluable autumn and winter flowering bulbs, which will be discussed later.

A number of the long-flowering summer perennials will often continue their display into early autumn, especially if regularly 'dead-headed' to prevent them going to seed. Dwarf *Aster novi-belgii* (Michaelmas daisy) varieties flower extremely freely during autumn and are good for bold colour masses in the border front. And the autumn-flowering schizostylis varieties are extremely useful for their bright red and pink gladiolus-like spikes.

Hardy fuchsias generally flower well into autumn in a mild season, and the dwarf variety 'Tom Thumb' is superb for low-growing colour (see 'Small Shrubs').

Popular choices for winter are the glistening white-flowered Christmas rose, *Helleborus niger*, and the lenten roses, *H. orientalis* varieties, mentioned earlier for winter-spring colour. *H. niger* needs a sheltered spot to protect its flowers from harsh winter weather, and a pane of glass or a cloche popped over it as the buds burst will further help to keep them immaculate.

And another firm favourite for winter flowers, in as well-drained and sunny a spot as possible (at the base of a sunny wall is ideal), is *Iris unguicularis* (previously *I. stylosa*). The delicate and highly fragrant blooms range from pale lavender-blue to rich violet-blue, according to variety, and are lovely enough to make an ideal flower to pick for the house.

□ Small shrubs for borders □

Many of the dwarf shrubs recommended for rock gardens and raised beds will be equally happy in a well-drained border, and these neatest-growing types are ideal where growing room is strictly limited. In addition there are numerous small shrubs too large for rock gardens and raised beds but good space-savers for general border planting.

Note: Where a shrub name is mentioned and followed by * but little or no description is given, refer to Chapter 3 for further details.

■ *Spring*

One of the very loveliest and most elegant of small shrubs for late winter and early spring flowers is *Magnolia stellata*. This slow-growing shrub may eventually get rather large for the smallest of borders, but only after many years. Its winter buds, large and covered in a furry coating of grey hairs, are attractive to see on the bare branches, followed by fragrant star-shaped white flowers 8–10 cm (3–4 in) across before the new spring foliage unfurls.

The dwarf rhododendrons* recommended in Chapter 3 for rock gardens and raised beds will grow quite happily in well-drained borders, provided the soil is lime free. If your garden is limy, then the place for these spring-flowering beauties is in a specially-made peat bed. They prefer some shade during the day, but will grow in full sun if kept well watered during dry weather in spring and summer. And be sure to add plenty of moisture-retaining humus material (e.g. peat) to the planting site.

One stunning small species not mentioned in Chapter 3 (because it can make quite a wide little bush and its leaves and flower trusses are rather too big to look right alongside the daintiest rock plants) is *Rhododendron yakushimanum*. This is a superb low-growing border shrub, with clusters of large pink-flushed white bell-flowers. The young leaves which follow the flowers are a feature in themselves, covered with an attractive woolly white coating.

Other dwarf spring-flowering shrubs which are as good in borders as on rock gardens and raised beds (see Chapter 3 for more details) include the low-spreading broom *Cytisus × kewensis**, the fragrant *Daphne retusa**, and *Berberis × stenophylla* 'Corallina Compacta'*.

■ *Summer*

Genista lydia is a useful low-growing broom for masses of bright yellow flowers in late spring and early summer. But it can spread quite widely, so is not for the smallest borders.

The dwarf mock oranges *Philadelphus microphyllus* (single white flowers) and *P.* 'Manteau d'Hermine' (double, creamy-wite) are wonderful free-flowering shrubs for early summer, with a deliciously rich fragrance that will fill the garden.

Shrubby potentillas are favourite choices for non-stop summer-long flowering. The very neatest-growing ones, *Potentilla arbuscula* 'Beesii'* and *P. fruticosa* 'Mandschurica'*, are described in Chapter 3. Other good compact varieties include 'Elizabeth' (yellow), 'Red Ace' (orange-red), 'Daydawn' (pinkish-yellow), and 'Tilford Cream' (creamy-white).

Also good for non-stop flowering during summer are the smaller sun rose varieties. *Cistus* 'Sunset' (rich crimson flowers) and *C.* 'Silver Pink' (satin-pink with a yellow centre) are the most compact ones.

Other neat-growing and long-flowering shrubs for summer include the compact lavender varieties 'Hidcote' (violet flower spikes) and 'Munstead' (rich lavender-blue), the *Erica cinerea** varieties (summer-flowering heathers), the violet-blue flowered *Hebe* 'Carl Teschner'*, and of course the wide range of miniature roses now commonly available from garden centres and shops (trim these back as the display fades, to encourage repeat flowering in late summer and early autumn).

The hardy fuchsia varieties also flower over an exceptionally long period during summer, and well into autumn if the weather stays mild. 'Mrs Popple' is a lovely small shrub, producing an endless display of red and purple flowers. And the very dwarf 'Tom Thumb' (red and pink) is ideal for the front of the border (or as a colourful edging).

Summer-flowering heathers, *Calluna vulgaris* varieties (see 'Conifer and heather beds' later in this chapter), are especially useful for late colour, generally flowering from late summer through into autumn. Remember that these and the other common summer heathers, the *Erica cinerea* varieties, need lime-free soil or a non-limy peaty planting mixture.

■ *Autumn and winter*

As I have said, you can depend on a number of the long-flowering and late-flowering summer shrubs continuing into autumn. As its name suggests, the violet-flowered *Hebe* 'Autumn Glory' is especially good in this respect, providing colour from summer virtually to autumn's end.

For additional colour in this season, the blue autumn flowers of *Caryopteris × clandonensis* are useful. The variety 'Heavenly Blue' is more compact and a richer blue. *Ceratostigma plumbaginoides* is a low ground-covering shrub, also with blue autumn flowers. *C. willmottianum* is similar but taller and bushier.

The tidy little winter heathers recommended for rock gardens and raised beds, the long-flowering varieties of *Erica herbacea* (syn. *E. carnea*)*, are obvious choices for winter-spring colour. Much larger (so not suitable for planting with alpines, but vigorous ground-cover for borders) are the *E. × darleyensis* varieties, some of which start their season well before Christmas. Best for such early colour are 'Arthur Johnson' (rose pink flowers), 'Darley Dale' (purple-pink) and 'Silberschmelze' or 'Silver Beads' (white).

For red autumn and winter berries, there is *Skimmia reevesiana*. The white flowers appear in late spring. Does best in lime-free soil.

And finally, one of the classic winter-flowering shrubs, the sweetly scented purple-red flowered *Daphne mezereum*. The flowers, which smother the bare winter branches, are followed by bright red berries (beware: these are poisonous). Equally lovely is the white-flowered form 'Alba', with amber-yellow berries.

■ *Shrubs for foliage effect*

The small Japanese maple varieties recommended in Chapter 3 for larger rock gardens and raised beds, *Acer palmatum* 'Dissectum'* and *A. p.* 'Dissectum Atropurpureum'*, are enchanting, slow-growing foliage shrubs for borders. They dislike summer drought, so give them plenty of peat, leafmould or compost in the soil. Just as charming is the faster-growing *A. p.* 'Atro-purpureum', with less deeply-divided leaves, rich purple in summer, turning

Roscoea cautleiodes, *a beautiful small perennial with orchid-like summer flower spikes.*

crimson-purple in autumn. This one will eventually grow into a small tree, but remains shrub-size for many years first.

Salix lanata* is easy-growing and valuable for its silvery-grey leaves, while the dwarf forms of *Berberis thunbergii* provide rich foliage colours for summer and autumn. *B. t.* 'Atropurpurea Nana' has rich purple leaves and is good as a single specimen or as a low hedge. *B. t.* 'Aurea' is larger, with bright yellow foliage.

Both the winter- and summer-flowering groups of heathers, of course, include varieties with bright evergreen foliage tints of gold, orange-red and bronze for year-round interest; especially useful for colour during the winter months. And the silvery-white and golden variegated forms of *Euonymus fortunei* are popular for low-spreading ground cover.

Meconopsis cambrica *is a free-seeding small perennial, good for non-stop summer colour in shady and dry borders.*

The smallest dwarf conifers listed in Chapter 3 for rock gardens and raised beds are suitable for well-drained soil in the tiniest of borders, and the larger types recommended there are equally at home in borders of all sizes, as small foliage shrubs. Especially good for colourful foliage in borders are *Chamaecyparis pisifera* 'Plumosa Aurea Nana'* (soft yellow foliage) and *Thuja occidentalis* 'Rheingold'* (rich old-gold tints).

Other small conifers not listed earlier (too large for most rock gardens and raised beds) but good for bushy or low-spreading evergreen interest in borders, include: *Chamaecyparis lawsoniana* 'Ellwood's Gold' (a fairly slow-growing upright conifer with yellow-tinged foliage), *C. pisifera* 'Boulevard' (bushy, with soft-steel-blue foliage), and the low ground-covering spreaders *Juniperus communis* 'Depressa Aurea' (golden young foliage), *J. procumbens* 'Nana' (rich green) and *J. squamata* 'Blue Carpet' (silvery-blue).

Finally, *Buxus sempervirens* 'Suffruticosa' is the dwarf, evergreen box that you should look out for if you want to give a border a neat and formal trimmed box-edging. This is also good as a low dividing hedge within the garden, and fine even as an untrimmed dwarf evergreen bush in a small border.

□ Dwarf bulbs for borders □

Dwarf bulbs are invaluable for packing borders with additional seasonal colour for spring and (more importantly) for the quiet months of autumn and winter. They also tend to be rather more elegant and charming than many of the taller and larger-flowered types of border bulb (as is always the case with miniature plants).

Note: Where a bulb is named and followed by * but little or no description is given, refer to Chapter 3 for more information.

■ Winter

This is the season when borders are most in need of a colourful boost, and the miniature bulbs recommended for early flowers on rock gardens and raised beds are just as useful here.

Do, however, make sure that you give these (and the tiniest bulbs for spring and autumn colour) well-drained conditions in the border. If the soil is at all heavy or (worse still) clayey, then work plenty of coarse sand into the planting site, plus some peat or other humus material. Without this drainage-improving and soil-lightening preparation, many of the smallest bulbs are prone to rotting-off in heavy soils during wet winter weather.

Do not, as is sometimes suggested, sit the bulbs in their planting holes on a layer of pure sand. Following heavy rain, water will simply drain into this sand layer from the surrounding soil, making the bases of the bulbs (the most vulnerable part; where the roots emerge) more waterlogged than ever. Instead, thoroughly mix the sand into the base of the planting hole, and into the soil you will be using for filling-in.

Good choices for early colour, from mid-winter to the first days of spring, are *Cyclamen coum**, *Crocus laevigatus**, *C. ancyrensis* ('Golden Bunch')*, *C. imperati**, *C. flavus**, *C. sieberi**, *Galanthus nivalis* (common snowdrop)*, *G. elwesii* (Turkish snowdrop)*, *Eranthis hyemalis* (winter aconite)* and *Anemone blanda**.

The dwarf irises, *Iris danfordiae**, *I. historioides* 'Major'*, and the varieties of *I. reticulata**, are also very early-flowering and extremely showy little bulbs. These need especially well-drained conditions and enjoy a summer baking in dry soil; so give them as sun-baked a spot as possible, and work lashings of coarse sand into the soil if it is at all heavy.

Taller growing than these but still very compact, ideal for small borders, and flowering in late winter, the dwarf *Narcissus cyclamineus* hybrids 'February Gold' (rich yellow), 'February Silver' (milky-white and lemon-yellow) and 'Tete-a-Tete' (very dwarf with two or more golden flowers to a stem) are excellent small trumpet daffodils for early colour.

■ Spring

A number of other beautiful dwarf trumpet daffodils flower in the first days of spring, or (in a mild season) from the last days of winter into early spring. Look out, in particular, for *N. cyclamineus* hybrids 'Dove Wings' (ivory-white with yellow trumpet) and 'Jack Snipe' (very low-growing, cream and primrose-yellow).

The early-flowering, easy-growing and very free-flowering *Crocus chrysanthus** varieties thrive in well-drained borders, as do the other miniature spring crocus recommended in Chapter 3 for rock gardens and raised beds.

Also very easy and free-flowering are the lilac-blue and purple-mauve forms of *C. tomasinianus*. This is especially good for naturalizing beneath deciduous shrubs; as are many of the most miniature winter, spring and autumn-flowering bulbs.

For splashes of bright blue in the early spring border, there are the chionodoxas*, *Scilla bifolia**, *S. tubergeniana** and *S. sibirica* 'Spring Beauty' (very rich deep blue). And for more brilliant blue flowers a little later in the season, choose *Ipheion uniflorum* 'Wisley Blue'.

The dainty *Narcissus triandrus* hybrids are charming dwarf daffodils with elegant dangling short-cupped flowers, produced later than the equally lovely dwarf *N. cyclamineus* trumpet types; so excellent for continuing the spring display. Look for 'April Tears' (very dainty, golden-yellow), 'Thalia' and 'Tresamble' (both pure white).

The late spring display would not be complete without tulips. Good easy-growing dwarf types ideal for small borders, or for frontal plantings in any size of border, include: *Tulip fosteriana* 'Princeps' and 'Cantata' (bright reds), *T. greigii* hybrids (scarlet-red or yellow, with handsome purple-striped leaves), *T. praestans* 'Fusilier' and 'Tubergen's Variety' (three or more hot orange-red flowers to a stem) and *T. tarda* (very dwarf, yellow-centred white star-shaped flowers very freely produced).

For earlier colour, from late winter to early spring, choose the very short-stemmed varieties of the waterlily tulip, *T. kaufmanniana*.

SPRING BULBS FOR SHADY BORDERS Virtually all the bulbs mentioned so far for winter and spring colour do best in sunny borders. The following are good choices for shadier spots (although all will thrive in full sun if given plenty of humus in the soil): the various erythronium species (graceful lilac-pink, white or yellow lily-like flowers with recurving petals, above leaves which are often handsomely marbled maroon or red-brown), *Fritillaria meleagris* (the snake's head fritillary; nodding white or purple bells), *Anemone nemorosa* (the wood anemone; creeping mats with white or blue flowers according to variety, including a pretty double white), *Leucojum vernum* (spring snowflake; white snowdrop-like bells, spotted green at the petal tips), *Eranthis hyemalis* (winter aconite)*, *Cyclamen coum**, *C. repandum** and *Galanthus nivalis* (common snowdrop). Larger-flowered varieties of the common snowdrop are available from specialist dwarf bulb nurseries and are well worth seeking out. The best and most widely available are *G. nivalis* 'Atkinsii' and *G. n.* 'S. Arnott'.

■ *Summer*

The vast majority of summer-flowering bulbs are tall-growing, so outside the scope of this book; although many are invaluable for exotic flowers during the summer months, especially the sumptuous lilies.

Worth mentioning, however, are the dinky *Gladiolus* 'Nanus' varieties. These are much smaller and more delicate than the usual tall-stemmed gladioli, so ideally suited to small borders. In areas with mild winters they may be left in the ground all year, but in colder regions they should be lifted for winter storage.

Among the low-growing bulbs ideal for summer colour (see Chapter 3 for details) include *Oxalis adenophylla**, *Cyclamen europaeum* (syn. *C. purpurascens*)*, *Allium narcissiflorum**, *A. flavum* 'Minor'* and *A. oreophilum* (var. *ostrowskianum*; bright pink).

Miniature roses provide a long summer display, especially if trimmed back to encourage repeat flowering when the first flush of blooms starts to fade.

■ *Autumn*

Like winter, this is a season when the additional colour that bulbs can provide in the border is extremely welcome.

All the hardy cyclamen and autumn-flowering crocus species and varieties described in Chapter 3 for rock gardens and raised beds are equally valuable for late flowers in borders. These include *Cyclamen neapolitanum* (syn. *C. hederifolium*) and *C. n.* 'Album'*, *C. cilicium*, *Crocus zonatus* (syn. *C. kotschyanus*)*, *C. goulimyi*, *C. medius*, *C. nudiflorus** and *C. speciosus**.

The other major group of autumn bulbs is the colchicums (often wrongly referred to as autumn crocus). Do not place these too close to small plants which may be swamped by the colchicums' coarse, flopping foliage. The showiest and most widely available types are *Colchicum speciosum* (crimson-purple, lilac-pink or white according to the variety), *C.* 'Violet Queen' (deep purplish violet), *C.* 'The Giant' (extra-large lilac-mauve goblets) and *C.* 'Waterlily' (large rosy-lilac double flowers). The white and pink forms of *C. autumnale* are less striking but dainty smaller-flowered types.

PEAT BEDS AND CONIFER/HEATHER BEDS

In addition to ordinary garden borders, peat beds and conifer-and-heather beds are popular features which lend themselves well to the gardening-in-miniature approach. The smaller the area you are able to give over to these, obviously, the more sense it makes to fill them with the neatest-growing plants available, so that you can squeeze as much variety and interest as possible into your limited growing space. Peat beds, in particular, can be expensive to create on a large scale, so tend to be quite small and ideal candidates for tidy-growing plant choices.

□ The peat bed □

Should your garden soil be limy, then a peat bed will allow you to grow a range of beautiful lime-hating plants, such as the rhododendrons, which would not survive for long in the ordinary borders.

But even if the garden soil is non-limy, a peat bed is still well worth considering because it will provide the ideal well-drained but humus-rich and moist root conditions that all lime-hating plants enjoy. It will also ideally suit various other plants which do not mind limy conditions but do like a 'spongy' humus-filled soil, which will not dry out too quickly in spring and summer.

■ *The site*
The peat bed should be sited where it will receive some shade during the day. This will suit the majority of the plants that may be grown in it, and reduces the need for artificial watering. However, it should not be overhung in any way (by tree branches, for example) but should have clear sky above; so that, although protected from the sun's direct rays for at least part of the day, it will still get

plenty of overhead daylight and will not be dark or gloomy.

Overhanging branches will also mean dripping rain in winter and wet fallen leaves in autumn, both of which (just as on the rock garden or raised bed) can quickly spell death to small and miniature plants.

And, again as for the rock garden or raised bed, the site ideally should be well sheltered rather than exposed to blustery winds which will dry the peaty growing mixture and desiccate sensitive leaves in spring and summer.

Naturally, the ideal site combining all these factors may not be easy to find in all gardens, but the closer you can get to these requirements, the better the results will be.

■ Soil

The next task, after choosing your site, is to check whether the soil is limy or not (if you do not already know). Simple-to-use pH testing kits can be had from garden shops for this purpose. If the soil is lime-free (neutral to acid on the testing kit scale) then site preparation is simply a matter of working in lashings of peat, plus coarse sand or non-limy grit for improved drainage.

The planting mixture should consist of approximately equal parts (by bulk) of the top-soil, peat and either coarse sand or grit, all thoroughly mixed together. Where the soil is very heavy or clayey and slow-draining, then a little extra sand or grit may be added. And, conversely, if the soil is light and sandy or gravelly, then less sand or grit will be needed; but additional quantities of peat would be advisable.

Once prepared, the soil mixture may simply be levelled as an otherwise normal bed, or it may be mounded a little to form gentle slopes as for a rock garden. But do make sure that the mounding is not too high nor the slopes too steep, otherwise the upper parts may prove excessively fast-draining and quickly become parched during spells of hot, dry weather; which peat garden plants will not appreciate.

If your garden soil is limy, then it cannot be used in the peat bed planting mixture. Instead, you will have to make up a mix of roughly two-thirds peat to one-third of coarse sand or non-limy grit (measured by bulk) plus a dose of a lime-free compound fertilizer. Alternatively, mix the same proportions of sand or grit with 'ericaceous' potting compost (available from garden centres and shops) and omit the fertilizer.

■ Construction

A low, raised bed must then be constructed and filled with this mixture. It need not be very deep, since most peat-loving plants are fairly shallow-rooting. Even a layer just a few inches deep may do for small plants and shrubs, but really you should aim for a depth of at least 30 cm (1 ft).

The walls of the bed may be formed with rocks (but not limestone), bricks, blocks, timber or any other reasonably attractive material. A traditional choice to support the planting mixture is peat blocks (Fig. 9). These should be thoroughly soaked and then laid flat (not on their ends or their sides) in courses just like bricks. Use your planting mixture like mortar between the peat blocks as you build. Small plants may be inserted in gaps and crevices in these peat walls, just as in a dry stone retaining wall, and will root into the damp blocks. Remember to build the walls so that they slope backwards a little against the weight of planting mixture behind, for stability and to catch falling rain (which will help to ensure that the peat blocks stay moist).

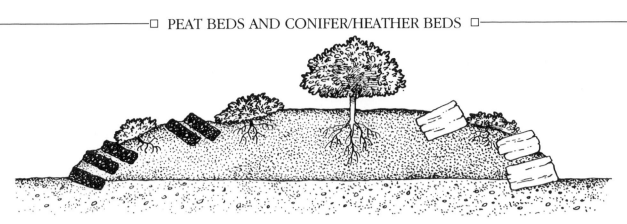

Fig. 9 Raised peat bed construction
The sides of a raised peat bed may be supported by walls of peat blocks (left-hand side
of drawing) or rocks (right-hand side). Terraces may also be created with peat block
walls or rockwork. Crevices between peat blocks or rocks may be planted, as on a rock
garden.

Rocks may be placed in peat beds for an attractive natural outcrop effect,
exactly as recommended in Chapter 2 for rock gardens and raised beds; but
make sure they are a non-limy type, such as sandstone. Alternatively, planting
terraces on varying levels may be created with a series of low peat-block walls
(the walls being planted as already suggested).

Finally, do not forget that if your tap-water is limy, then you should water
peat beds with non-limy rainwater.

■ *Plants for peat beds*
The dwarf rhododendrons recommended in Chapter 3 for rock gardens and
raised beds are obvious choices for peat bed culture. So, too, are the exotic
blue trumpet-flowered autumn gentians discussed in the same chapter; indeed,
a well-made peat bed in semi-shade is the ideal situation for these stunning but
rather tricky little plants.

Dwarf evergreen azaleas will also be happy here although, as I said earlier,
their flower colourings tend to be rather garish to associate well with the more
refined and elegant charms of many other miniature plants and shrubs; and I
would rather see these planted on their own in tubs.

Heathers of all kinds will thrive in a peaty planting mixture. Virtually all the
summer-flowering types, including the popular *Calluna vulgaris* and *Erica
cinerea* varieties, must have lime-free conditions. Even the lime-tolerant,
winter-flowering heathers, the varieties of *E. herbacea* (syn. *E. carnea*) and
E. × darleyensis, will grow better in a non-limy peaty planting mix. (See
'Conifer and heather beds' next in this chapter, and Chapter 3, for further
information on these and other types of heather).

Here are a few suggestions to help you choose peat-bed plants. Some are
lime-haters, others just like moist humus-rich soil and a little shade. You will
find many more in the catalogues of specialist rock plant nurseries.

SHRUBS
Andromeda polifolia (creeping shrublet, pink bell flowers)
Cassiope lycopodioides (white lily-of-the-valley-like flowers)
Gaultheria cuneata (white flowers and berries)
Heathers (all types)
Pernettya tasmanica (large red autumn berries)
Continued on p. 88

Above: *Dwarf rhododendrons are obvious choices for small peat beds; seen here, a compact-growing* Rhododendron yakushimanum *hybrid.*

Opposite: *For the larger peat bed, the blue 'Himalayan poppy'* Meconopsis betonicifolia *is a stunning choice.*

Phylodoce empetriformis (bright rose-pink flowers)
P. nipponica (white flowers)
Polygala chamaebuxus (yellow pea-like flowers)
Rhododendron (all dwarf types)
Vaccinium caespitosum (pink or white flowers).

PLANTS
Anemone nemorosa (white or blue flowers)
Cyananthus lobatus (violet-blue)
Dodecatheon media (pink cyclamen-like flowers)
Gentiana sino-ornata and other autumn-flowering gentians (blue trumpets)
Glaucidium palmatum (lavender poppy-flowers)
Iris innominata (yellow) and its hybrid offspring (variously coloured)
Lewisia cotyledon hybrids (shades of pink or apricot)
Meconopsis betonicifolia (blue Himalayan poppy; tall, but superb for larger peat beds)
Ramonda myconi (lavender-blue)
Sanguinaria canadensis 'Flore Pleno' (snow-white double flowers)
Trillium grandiflorum (white flowers).

BULBS
Erythronium (all types; lily-like pink, yellow or white flowers)
Cyclamen (all hardy species)
Fritillaria meleagris (white or purple bells)
Narcissus cyclamineus (tiny yellow trumpets).

For an example of a small peat bed planting scheme see Fig. 10.

□ The conifer and heather bed □

Due to the dense ground-covering and weed-suppressing nature of heathers (and of spreading conifers) this is a very easy-to-maintain garden feature, requiring little weeding or working once established. It also allows the gardener to create attractive miniature heathland landscape effects with trees rising above low-growing heather carpets and outcrops of craggy rockwork.

A sunny site is essential for free flowering, and you should prepare the ground as for a peat bed, to ensure the well-drained but moist conditions in which heathers thrive. If the garden soil is limy, then construct a low raised bed filled with lime-free planting mixture on the lines set out in the previous section of this chapter. This will enable you to grow the lime-hating summer heathers as well as the lime-tolerant winter-flowering types, for colour and interest throughout the year.

Rock outcrops may be constructed, for additional effect, in the same way as recommended for rock gardens and raised beds. Be sure to use a non-limy rock, and take care to plant only the lowest-growing types of heather – generally the winter-flowering *Erica herbacea* (syn. *E. carnea*) varieties – around the rocks so that your outcrops will not be swamped and hidden by tall-growing foliage.

For this reason, it is even more important than on the rock garden to go for a few large rocks rather than lots of smaller ones, which would be more easily lost in a sea of spreading heathers. Indeed, one large outcrop, built up to a fair

Fig. 10 Small peat bed example planting scheme

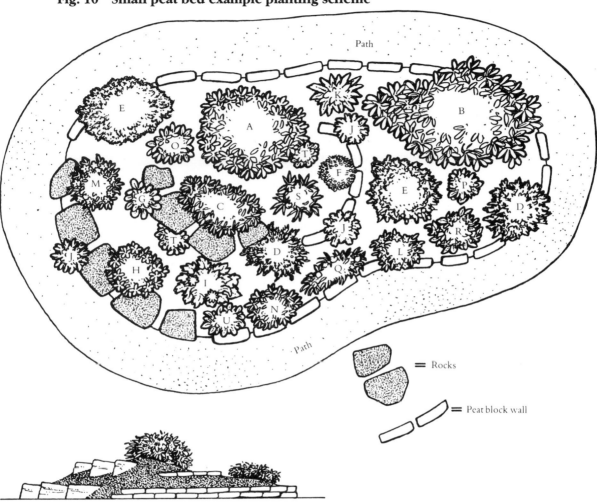

= Rocks

= Peat block wall

Shrubs
(A) bushy dwarf rhododendron variety; (B) low-spreading rhododendron variety; (C) *Polygala chamaebuxus*; (D) *Erica carnea* varieties; (E) *E. cinerea* varieties; (F) *Cassiope lycopodioides*.

Plants
(G) *Ramonda myconi*; (H) *Cyananthus lobatus*; (I) *Sanguinaria canadensis* 'Flore Pleno'; (J) *Lewisia cotyledon* hybrids; (K) *Roscoea cautleoides*; (L) *Gentiana sino-ornata*; (M) *G. macaulayi* 'Kingfisher'; (N) *Anemone nemorosa* variety (e.g. the blue-flowered 'Allenii'); (O) *Trillium grandiflorum*; (P) *Dodecatheon media*.

Bulbs
(Q) *Fritillaria meleagris*; (R) *Erythronium* variety (e.g. 'White Beauty' or the yellow-flowered 'Pagoda'); (S) *Narcissus cyclamineus*; (T) *Cyclamen coum*; (U) *C. hederifolium* (*neapolitanum*).

height (and perhaps with one or two suitable rock plants or neat-growing heathers planted in the soil-filled crevices), will be much more effective amongst the bushy mats of heathers than a number of smaller outcrops.

Above: *Californian iris hybrids enjoy the lime-free growing conditions of a peat bed.*

Opposite: Erythronium 'White Beauty'; *the erythroniums grow well in the humus-rich conditions offered by a peat bed.*

■ *Planting and maintenance*

The first priority should be to ensure colour and interest in every season. Choose heather varieties to flower at different times, bearing in mind that even within the two main groups of winter and summer heathers the flowering periods vary from one type to another. By careful selection you can extend the display in both cases to provide almost continuous year-round flowering.

Additional constant colour is easily arranged with evergreen conifers and heathers, by including varieties with bright foliage tints. But do not go overboard with colourful foliage effects, otherwise the bed may end up looking too contrived and artificial; a veritable patchwork quilt of different hues.

For a more subtle and natural effect, green foliage (in varying shades) should predominate, with the odd patch of brighter foliage here and there, to provide contrast and permanent colour. Also, some of the brighter-leaved heathers tend to flower rather less freely than the plainer-leaved types, so this is another good reason not to flood a small heather bed with them.

Aim for variety in plant heights and forms, just as you would in any other garden planting. An upright, column-shaped conifer or two will obviously provide the greatest and most pleasing contrast to the spreading mats of heather. But bushy conifers, too, can play a role and there are many of this type which boast excellent foliage tints. And amongst the heathers themselves there is quite a variety of height and shape. Including some of the taller and bushier types will introduce further variety and contrast into the planting scheme.

Where there is plenty of space to play with, a spreading conifer or two will

add further variety of foliage shape and colour. But in a small bed these space-hungry conifers are better excluded and the growing room given over to more interesting flowering heathers.

The best times to plant are spring and autumn. Set the heathers deep, burying the stems so that the foliage rests on the soil. Space the neatest-growing types about 30 cm (1 ft) apart, the taller and wider-spreading varieties at about 45 cm (1½ ft). In a large bed, grouping together a number of plants of the same variety will produce very bold and effective drifts of colour, but where space is strictly limited single specimens of each variety may well have to be used instead.

As for maintenance, keep well watered during dry weather in spring and summer (using rainwater for lime-hating summer heathers if your tap-water is limy) and top-dress annually with peat. Trim the old flower-heads of summer heathers in spring, and lightly cut back winter and spring varieties after flowering to keep them compact.

■ *Choosing heathers and conifers*

The popular column-shaped *Chamaecyparis lawsoniana* 'Elwoodii' and *C. l.* 'Elwood's Gold' are largish upright-growing conifers suitable for fairly spacious beds (although both are slow-growing at first, and will be all right even in a small bed for a number of years). *Taxus baccata* 'Standishii' is slower and makes a neat golden-leaved column ideal for more restricted spaces.

Very tiny dwarf conifers are not ideal choices, since they are likely to be overrun by the more vigorous heathers. But the less dwarf types described in Chapter 3 for rock gardens and raised beds are suitable. The best of these bushy and cone-shaped conifers include *Chamaecyparis pisifera* 'Boulevard' (silvery-blue), *C. p.* 'Plumosa Aurea Nana' (golden-yellow), *Picea glauca* 'Albertiana Conica' (green), *Thuja occidentalis* 'Rheingold' (rich amber-gold), and *T. o.* 'Sunkist' (bright yellow).

The neatest-growing winter- and spring-flowering heathers, the *Erica herbacea* (syn. *E. carnea*) varieties, are described in Chapter 3. These generally provide colour from mid-winter to early spring and will tolerate limy soil. Still more long-flowering (though also larger and more vigorous) are the *E. × darleyensis* types described in Chapter 5 for border planting. These bloom from early winter to spring, extending the season; they are also lime-tolerant. The *E. mediterranea* varieties are tall and bushy, spring-flowering heathers, which tolerate lime in the soil. Compact choices include 'Brightness' (rose-purple), 'Irish Salmon' (pink) and 'W.T. Rackliff' (white).

Most compact-growing of the summer heathers are the *E. cinerea* varieties listed and described in Chapter 3, flowering from early summer to early autumn. The more vigorous *Calluna vulgaris* types start their display later and continue further into autumn, extending the season. Good choices include 'Golden Carpet' (gold foliage, purple flower spikes), 'H.E. Beale' (double pink), 'Kinlochruel' (double white flowers, very dark foliage), 'Peter Sparkes' (double pink), 'Robert Chapman' (purple flowers; gold, orange and red foliage tints) and 'Silver Queen' (purple flowers, grey foliage). Both these and the *Erica cinerea* types need lime-free soil.

You will find others in some catalogues, such as the lime-hating and tall growing *Daboecia cantabrica* varieties, with large bell-flowers in rich shades of crimson and purple. But those listed here are the staples of the conifer and heather bed.

CHAPTER SEVEN

DWARF BULBS IN GRASS

Trumpet daffodils and large-flowered Dutch crocus naturalized in grass are a traditional feature of larger gardens. But what we are looking at here is a neater miniature-bulb feature more suited to an ordinary-size (or even small) lawn.

You need only choose a small patch of turf, perhaps adjoining a rock garden, raised bed, or other miniature garden with which the dwarf bulbs will be in scale, and which they will complement; or an out-of-the-way corner, maybe under a tree where the grass grows thinly anyway, and where some planting would make a handsome feature of an otherwise balding and ugly piece of turf.

Even with just a handful of bulbs in a square foot or two of grass, you can create a pretty little scene which will add interest to the garden at the appropriate season. And on a grander scale, a whole range of tiny spring and autumn bulbs may be planted, to spangle the turf with bright and dainty flowers for a delightful alpine lawn effect.

▢ Planting ▢

If you are laying or seeding a new lawn, then planting the bulbs in advance will obviously be no problem. With an established lawn, take out circles of turf with a trowel or bulb-planting tool; or cut, skim and roll-back squares of grass.

The second option allows you to do some thorough soil improvement, adding coarse sand and peat if the soil is heavy and slow-draining, plus a little compound fertilizer. On dry sandy or gravelly soils, add peat and fertilizer only. Even if you are only taking out small planting circles, try to work some sand and peat into the bottom of the hole with the point of the trowel, to improve the drainage a little on heavy soils. This is not as vital as it is when planting small bulbs in borders, since the root action of the turf will help somewhat in preventing the bulbs from getting too waterlogged. But if the lawn tends to be wet and muddy for long periods during winter, then anything you can do to improve the drainage before planting the bulbs will be well worth the effort.

Do not plant miniature bulbs too deeply; their noses need only be about

Narcissus *'February Gold'*, *an early-flowering dwarf trumpet daffodil ideal for naturalizing in grass.*

2.5–4 cm (1–1½ in) below the surface. A top-dressing of a long-lasting compound fertilizer in autumn or late winter each year will help to keep them growing and flowering strongly. And do remember to mow around the leaves in spring and early summer, only cutting the grass when the bulb foliage has yellowed. This may sound rather inconvenient, but many miniature bulbs die down earlier than tall trumpet daffodils; and having to tolerate a little patch of unmown grass for a few weeks is a small price to pay for such a charming effect. Indeed, if it is an out-of-the-way corner, or around the base of a tree, then you will hardly notice it anyway.

□ Bulbs to choose □

Note: Where a bulb name is mentioned and followed by an asterisk * but little or no description is given, refer to Chapter 3 for further details.

Crocus are obvious choices for spring colour, and their leaves die down early so do not get in the way of mowing for too long. The blue, yellow, cream and white varieties of *Crocus chrysanthus** listed in Chapter 3 are excellent, strong-growing and very free-flowering. *Crocus ancyrensis* (deep yellow) and *C. flavus* (orange-yellow) are also good choices, and the very easy-growing lilac-blue and purple forms of *C. tomasinianus* do especially well in grass; even in very dry patches around the trunks of trees.

The tiny hoop-petticoat daffodil, *Narcissus bulbocodium** will naturalize well

Cyclamen hederifolium (neapolitanum) *naturalizes well in short grass, even in very dry areas beneath trees.*

in short grass, and so will the little trumpet-flowered *N. cyclamineus** if planted in a semi shaded spot where it will not get too baked in summer (also a good choice for moist, mossy areas of grass). Also good for shadier and moister corners are *Fritillaria meleagris* (large white or purple bells), *Galanthus nivalis* (common snowdrop), *Eranthis hyemalis* (the yellow winter aconite), and *Cyclamen coum** (also good in sunnier areas, but will appreciate lots of peat in the soil to prevent it drying out too much in summer).

Other miniature spring bulbs suitable for planting in short grass (all best, like the crocus and hoop-petticoat daffodil, in sunny spots) include the bright blue chionodoxas* and scillas*, and the blue, pink, magenta-red and white varieties of *Anemone blanda*.

The *Narcissus cyclamineus* hybrids 'February Gold' and 'February Silver' are taller growing, but still very neat little trumpet daffodils (much smaller than the more usual large-flowered types). These are good where a bolder display is desired, and where larger and longer-lasting bulb leaves will not be a problem in the grass; such as around the base of a tree.

For autumn colour, the pink and white forms of *Cyclamen neapolitanum* (syn. *C. hederifolium*)* are marvellous. This will grow happily in sun or shade, and will even thrive in parched turf right at the base of a tree (although here it should be given plenty of peat). Also good for this season are the autumn crocus. Among the suitable choices here include *Crocus medius* (mauve-purple), *C. nudiflorus* (rich purple) and the strong-growing and very free-flowering *C. speciosus* (various shades of blue).

CHAPTER EIGHT

MINIATURE PLANTS IN CONTAINERS

Miniature plants, shrubs and bulbs are of course ideally suited to container planting, and this is where some of the most enchanting and truly tiny mini-gardens may be created.

Trough and sink gardens are very popular, but equally delightful miniature gardens may be conjured up in a range of other containers, including wooden tubs, large pots and pans, and even window boxes.

▫ The containers ▫

The one essential that any container must have, if it is to be planted-up as a permanent mini-garden, is adequate drainage holes in the base. If these are too small then they may easily become clogged, and if there are too few of them to cope with the volume of the container, than drainage will be slow and the plants will suffer. This is much more important where highly drainage-sensitive plants such as alpines and dwarf bulbs are to be grown than if the container was to be filled with temporary bedding plants.

If in doubt, enlarge the drainage holes and/or make more of them, since you can never have too much drainage but too little may prove disastrous. In large containers like troughs, tubs and more spacious window boxes, the holes should be at least 2 cm (¾ in) in diameter, and should ideally be spaced across the base at 10–15 cm (4–6 in) intervals.

Avoid highly ornate or brightly-coloured containers which will clash with the quiet charm and elegance of many miniature plants. Natural stone, neutral-coloured reconstructed stone, dark stained wood, and unglazed terracotta containers are far more suitable and unobtrusive.

Old stone sinks and troughs make the loveliest planting containers of all, especially when well weathered, with a handsome covering of mosses and lichens. But unfortunately these now fetch prohibitive prices. Specialist alpine nurseries can sometimes supply them (generally for collection only) if you can afford the price tag.

Reconstructed stone troughs can prove an acceptable substitute, but some look decidedly more realistic than others; so do shop around and go for those which approximate most closely to the real thing (and, preferably, without ostentatious ornamentation). The one real problem with reconstructed stone is that it tends to weather more slowly than natural stone. Painting a few times, after planting, with a strong solution of organic liquid manure (e.g. seaweed

Fig. 11 Making a hyper-tufa trough in a wooden box mould

(*a*)   Place the outer box mould on a plastic sheet and place 5 cm (2 in) pots inside, to support the inner mould.

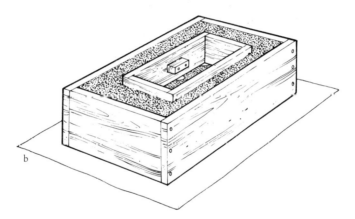

(*b*)   Fill the base with hyper-tufa mixture (see text), position the inner mould, then pack hyper-tufa mixture into the 5–6 cm (2–2½ in) gap between the inner and outer boxes.

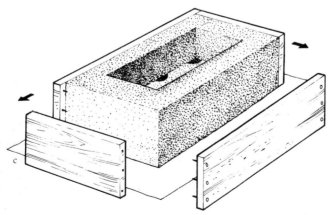

(*c*)   When the mixture is firm, remove the inner box and the small pots (to leave drainage holes); once hardened, gently prise apart and remove the outer box.

Above: *Old stone troughs and sinks make wonderful containers for miniature gardens but are rather pricey these days.*

Opposite: *Tufa is a light porous rock ideal for container gardens, since alpines may be planted into it, as here.*

manure), and regularly wetting the outer surfaces during dry weather, will tone the colour down a little and encourage moss and lichen growth.

The half-barrels commonly available from garden centres make attractive containers for miniature gardens and are less expensive than either stone or imitation-stone troughs. They also have another factor in their favour: planting holes may easily be drilled and cut into their sides, to provide snug homes for the rosette-forming and trailing rock plants which look good in such positions; and which, in some cases, enjoy the protection from winter rains that a vertical planting site offers.

The largest sizes of terracotta pots and pans available from garden centres make handsome containers for the choicest mini-gardens. They look a real treat on a small patio, planted with one of the tiniest of dwarf conifers and a handful of the daintiest alpines, plus a mossy stone or two arranged as a miniature rock outcrop.

As for window boxes, choose plain stained wood rather than plastic, for its natural appearance and for its insulating properties against winter cold and the heat of the sun in summer. Certainly avoid highly decorated boxes which may look fine filled with riotously-colourful summer annuals, but which will jar with the more subtle attractions of a permanent mini-garden planting scheme. And if the boxes must be painted rather than stained, make the colour as neutral as possible for the same reason.

■ *Home-made troughs*

An attractive, and satisfying, alternative to expensive stone troughs and rather stark-looking concrete or reconstructed stone containers is to make your own. This is quite easy to do, and great fun, too.

Rock plant enthusiasts originated a method of making lightweight troughs which weather and age quickly, using a mixture of sand, cement and peat now commonly known as hypertufa (named after a soft porous rock in which alpines can actually be grown; but more on this fascinating subject later).

The point of adding a large helping of peat is that it slightly darkens and tones-down the stark colouring of the sand-and-cement mix, and (just as importantly) the resulting porous-surfaced trough develops moss and lichen growths much faster than either plain concrete or reconstructed stone. As a result, the trough quickly takes on an aged and weathered natural appearance that complements and enhances the planting scheme.

All that is needed is two rectangular wooden boxes or plastic containers which will fit one inside the other, with a gap of 5–6 cm (2–2½ in) between them all round (Fig. 11). Even stout cardboard boxes will do, but these will have to be supported inside and out when filled with the sand-cement-peat mix. I have had the best results using plastic planters as moulds.

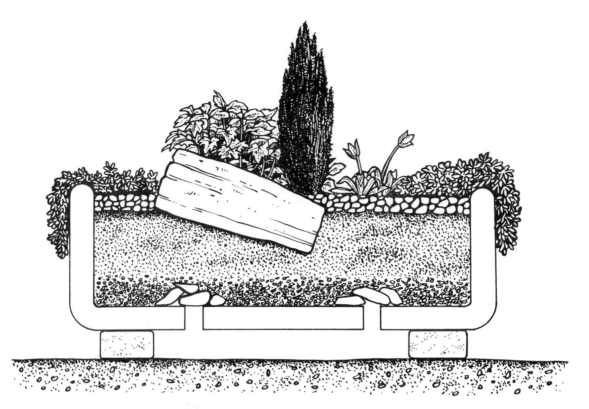

Fig. 12 Planting a container mini-garden
Cover the drainage holes with broken crocks or small stones, add a drainage layer of
grit or chippings, then fill in with well-drained soil mixture and top-dress with stone
chippings. Small rocks may be used in containers as recommended for rock gardens.
Support the container on bricks or stones.

Place small plastic plant pots upside-down in the larger box, to support the
smaller inner box with a gap of about 8 cm (3 in) between their bases (5 cm or
2 in pots are about the right size). Prepare a mix of one part cement to one part
sharp or coarse sand, and two parts moist peat (measured by bulk). Add water
until the consistency is firm and mouldable but not runny. Lift out the inner
box and fill the base of the larger (outer) box with mixture to the tops of the
small pots. Sit the inner box back onto the pots, making sure it is central, then
pack the gap between the sides of the two boxes with mixture. Tamp down
frequently to avoid air pockets.

After a few hours the mix should be set enough for you to gently remove the
inner box. After another 24–48 hours the hypertufa mixture should be hard
enough for you to carefully remove the outerbox. If using a wooden mould,
this may simply be prised apart, and a cardboard box will simply tear away. If
you are using a plastic container, you will have to gently tip the trough out onto
a cushioning layer of sacking or cardboard (two pairs of hands are best for this
tricky bit). Give the trough a further four or five days to harden completely
before planting.

While the trough is still not completely hardened, take the opportunity to
give it an aged and rough-hewn appearance, by carefully gouging out some
'chisel marks' and by rounding-off and smoothing-down sharp edges and
corners with a knife, wire brush and damp cloth. And at the same time, gently
knock out the small pots from the base, to leave drainage holes.

Finally, treat with a strong organic liquid manure solution, as recommended earlier for reconstructed stone troughs, to encourage moss and lichen growth.

□ Soil and planting □

Never use garden soil for plants in containers; it is likely to be full of weeds, disease spores and pests which will play havoc with plants in the confines of a container. And, in particular, never use unimproved garden soil, which may be clayey and slow-draining. Instead, for growing rock plants, dwarf conifers and shrubs, and miniature bulbs, make up a mix of roughly equal proportions (by bulk) of soil-based potting compost, peat, and grit or stone chippings. For lime-hating and peat-loving plants, mix two parts of lime-free ericaceous potting compost with one part (by bulk) of coarse sand or non-limy grit.

Cover the container's drainage holes with broken pieces of clay pot or small stones, to prevent clogging, then spread a layer of grit or chippings in the base. How deep you make this will depend on the depth of the container. About 5–8 cm (2–3 in) is usually quite adequate. But in a deep tub or trough it can be as much as a third of the available depth. In a very shallow container, on the other hand, there may only be room to spare for a sprinkling of grit or chippings to aid bottom-drainage. Fill-in above this with your planting mixture, firming down gently and ensuring that there are no air-pockets (Fig. 12).

Small rocks may be placed in containers in the same way as recommended for rock gardens and raised beds. Remember that they should tilt backwards so that they appear to rise up out of the soil like a miniature natural outcrop. Any type of rock will do (although you should avoid limestone where lime-hating plants are to be grown). However, one of the very best choices for containers is tufa. This is a lightweight, soft and porous rock available from some alpine nurseries by mail-order (or a local garden centre or landscape gardening firm might be able to obtain it for you). Holes may be cut into it and filled with soil mixture for tiny cushion- or rosette-forming alpines, which will eventually root into the soft rock.

This is a lovely way to grow some of the choicest rock plants and give them the extra well-drained root conditions that they demand. And it makes excellent use of the very limited room in a container garden.

A couple of words of warning, though. First, while lime-hating plants will sometimes grow in some types of tufa (for reasons of varying chemical composition too complex to go into here) this is basically a limy rock, so do not risk planting lime-haters in it. Secondly, avoid watering the rock and its plants from above, as this may encourage excessive moss growth on the porous rock surface. Keep the soil in the container well watered in dry weather, and the tufa will soak up from below the moisture that the plants need.

Planting procedures are as set out earlier for rock gardens and raised beds. Remember to top-dress the soil with chippings to conserve soil-moisture in dry weather, protect low-growing plants and delicate flowers from soil-splash, and give the mini-garden attractive finish. And do not forget to keep the container well watered while the plants become established, and thereafter do not let them go short of water during spring and summer.

The best way to feed plants in container-gardens is with two or three doses of liquid fertilizer during spring and early summer, since solid fertilizers tend to wash off in heavy rain. Use a high-potash feed to encourage free flowering and discourage excessive leafy growth.

Above: *Old stone troughs and sinks come in all shapes and sizes. Here a circular trough provides a cosy home for a range of rock plants.*

Opposite: *A beautifully planted range of trough gardens with a good mix of dwarf conifers, rock plants and miniature bulbs.*

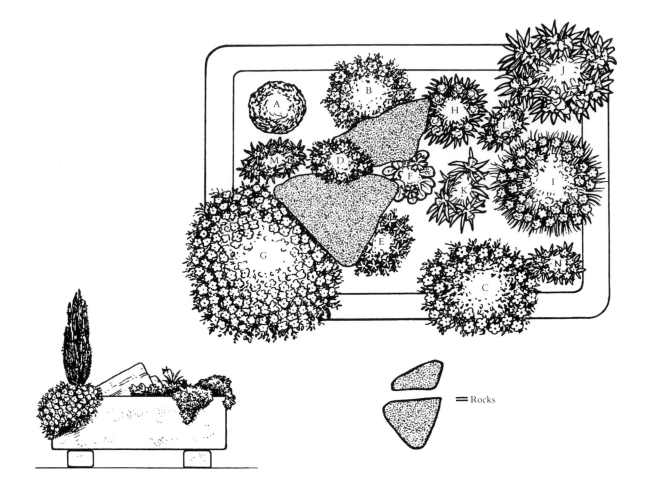

Fig. 13   Small container-garden example planting scheme

Trees
(A) *Juniperus communis* 'Compressa' or *Cryptomeria japonica* 'Vilmoriniana'.

Plants
(B) *Saxifraga* 'Cranbourne'; (C) *S. oppositifolia*; (D) *S. cochlearis* 'Minor'; (E) *Gentiana verna*; (F) *Primula auricula* 'Blairside Yellow'; (G) *Phlox douglasii* variety; (H) *Dianthus* 'Whitehills'; (I) *Armeria caespitosa*; (J) *Campanula haylodgensis* 'Flore Plena'.

Bulbs
(K) *Narcissus asturiensis*; (L) *Crocus minimus*; (M) *C. medius*; (N) *C. chrysanthus* variety.

□ Planting design □

The basics of good planting design apply as much to the tiniest container mini-garden as to the largest bed or border: ensure year-round interest by choosing plants for flowers in different seasons and evergreens for constant foliage effect (many alpines have handsome foliage, and dwarf conifers are of course especially useful for this purpose); and for variety of height and scale, include plants of varying sizes and growth habits.

A taller, upright-growing plant or two (such as a column-shaped dwarf conifer) is essential, to give the mini-garden height. Bushier plants will introduce bulk and provide a contrast to lower-growing mat and cushion plants, while trailers spilling over the sides of the container will add yet another dimension to the display and balance the tallest plants above.

Take care to choose plants to suit the site intended for the container garden. Remember that the general run of rock plants, dwarf conifers and shrubs, and miniature bulbs prefer a sunny situation. For a gloomier spot, select plants which enjoy or tolerate shade. Indeed, a shady site cries out for a selection of moisture-loving and lime-hating plants which like a peaty planting mixture and not too much sun.

And most importantly, be sure to carefully tailor your choice of plants to the size of the trough, tub, window box, pot or pan. Nowhere is this more vital than in container-gardening, where a single too-vigorous or invasive plant may easily swamp the entire miniature garden. An example of a planting plan for a small container garden is shown in Fig. 13.

□ Plants for container gardens □

Note: Where a plant name is given and followed by an asterisk * but little or no description is given, refer to Chapter 3 for further details.

■ *Trees and shrubs*

There is no lovelier or neater miniature deciduous tree for container gardens than the very slow-growing, gnarled and silvery-leaved dwarf willow *Salix × boydii**. This willl never outgrow the smallest trough, nor even the tiniest pot or pan mini-garden.

And the very best of the dwarf conifers is, without question, the extremely slow-growing and compact spire-shaped *Juniperus communis* 'Compressa'*. This is equally unlikely ever to get too large for the most diminutive container gardens. Other very neat-growing treasures suitable for small containers include the bushy little *Abies balsamea* 'Hudsonia'*, *Chamaecyparis obtusa* 'Nana' (a tiny dome of very dark black-green foliage), the mossy-leaved and ball-shaped *Cryptomeria japonica* 'Vilmoriniana'* and *Picea mariana* 'Nana' (forms a dense mound of grey-green foliage).

The following, less dinky types will provide a quicker effect in more spacious containers but may eventually get a little on the large side and need to be replaced with something smaller after a few years:
Chamaecyparis lawsoniana 'Minima Aurea'* (golden-yellow)
C. l. 'Pygmaea Argentea'* (green and white)
C. obtusa 'Nana Lutea' (golden) and *Picea abies* 'Nidiformis'* (green).

My favourite dwarf evergreen shrub for container planting is the slow-growing and sweetly scented *Daphne retusa**. In the open ground this delightful spring-flowering shrub may eventually grow quite large, but in the root-restricting confines of a container garden it remains compact for quite a number of years. In addition, the pink-flowered and equally fragrant *D. cneorum** is a good choice for the corner of a container, where its low-trailing branches may spread outwards.

Above: *The smallest varieties of the 'encrusted' saxifrages are excellent hummock-forming plants for container gardens.*

Opposite: *Container garden plantings should always include some trailing plants, to cascade attractively over the sides.*

A similar situation will suit the miniature trailing willow *Salix reticulata*, with its shiny green and handsomely vein-netted leaves (in a sunny situation, give this plenty of peat and keep well watered in dry weather).

*Cytisus ardoinii** is a very compact mat-forming dwarf broom, ideal for a splash of yellow during spring. For golden-yellow summer flowers, *Hypericum olympicum** is a pretty little grey-leaved evergreen bush which will stay tidy enough for a larger container if trimmed hard when the display ends. And *Penstemon roezlii* is a neat evergreen producing masses of bright carmine-pink snapdragon flowers from late spring to early summer.

Erica herbacea (syn. *E. carnea*)* varieties are neat-growing heathers valuable for winter colour. Particularly compact are 'Vivellii' (rich carmine-red flowers and handsome bronze-green foliage) and 'King George' (rose pink). Rather larger-growing, but the neatest of the summer-flowering heathers, are the *E. cinerea** varieties. The most compact choices for containers are 'Alba Minor' (white) and 'Pink Ice' (deep pink); do not forget that these need a lime-free planting mixture.

For container gardens in shady situations, the smallest dwarf rhododendrons recommended in Chapter 3 for rock gardens and raised beds are obvious candidates; provided you give them a lime-free planting mix of ericaceous peat potting compost and coarse sand or non-limy grit. Other good choices for a shady site and a peaty compost mixture include *Andromeda polifolia* (pink bells), *Cassiope lycopodioides* (white bell-flowers) and *Polygala chamaebuxus* (yellow pea-flowers).

■ Rock plants

Of the rock plants which form neat hummocks or tufts, the alpine primulas are excellent choices for spring flowers, notably the various lavender-blue forms of *Primula marginata**. Also good are the *P. × pubescens* varieties*, *P. auricula* 'Blairside Yellow' (very dainty, with yellow flowers) and *P.* 'Bileckii' (deep rose-pink).

For early summer flower spikes plus attractive silver-grey leaf rosettes, the hummock-forming 'encrusted' saxifrages are superb container-garden plants; especially the neatest types described in Chapter 3 for rock gardens and raised beds. The pink flowers of *Armeria caespitosa** provide useful and long-lasting colour around the same time, and this is another excellent choice; as are the summer-flowering *Geranium farreri* (syn. *G. napuligerum*)* (the only geranium species neat enough to recommend for small containers), *Sempervivum arachnoideum** and the charming *Campanula persicifolia* 'Planiflora Alba' (syn. *C. nitida* 'Alba') (short spikes of large white bell-flowers).

Most rock garden campanulas are too wide-spreading or invasive for troughs and other container gardens. Be wary of the dainty, mat-forming *C. cochleari-ifolia* which, although a beauty for rock gardens, raised beds, paving, etc., may quickly fill a container with its underground-creeping shoots. A beautiful and unusual alternative is the less vigorous *C. × haylodgensis* 'Flore Plena', a real charmer forming neat tufts with elegant little double flowers of clear lavender-blue.

For low-growing mats and early winter-spring colour, the kabschia saxifrages* are wonderful. In small container gardens avoid the most vigorous and wide-spreading ones, such as *Saxifraga × apiculata* and *S.* 'Elizabethae', and go instead for neater types like the *S. burserana* varieties (white or yellow), *S.* 'Cranbourne' (deep pink) and *S.* 'Jenkinsae' (shell-pink).

Other tidy mat-forming plants for mini-gardens in troughs, tubs, window boxes and pots include the spring-flowering *Gentiana verna** and *G. acaulis**, and the dainty alpine 'pinks' *Dianthus alpinus*', *D.* 'La Bourbrille'* and *D.* 'Whitehills'* for summer. Beware the popular *D. deltoides**, which is too fast-spreading and free-seeding for these tiniest of miniature-garden situations.

The *Phlox douglasii** varieties are easy-growing trailers to spill over the sides of larger containers, but avoid the more rampant *P. subulata* types. Other good trailers for the edges of troughs, etc., are *Saxifraga oppositifolia**, *Gentiana septemfida**, *Dryas octopetala* 'Minor' or *D. integrifolia* (syn. *D. tenella*) (white summer flowers, followed by fluffy seed heads).

Suitable choices for containers in shady sites and filled with a peaty compost include: *Gentiana sino-ornata** and other autumn-flowering gentians, *Cyananthus lobatus* (lilac-blue flowers), *Ramonda myconi**, *Lewisia cotyledon* hybrids*, and *Anemone nemorosa* (in its white, double-flowered white, or blue varieties).

■ *Bulbs, corms and tubers*

Miniature bulbs are useful for underplanting in container gardens, to provide extra seasonal colour in winter, spring and autumn. The dry summer resting conditions that most dwarf bulbs enjoy do not exactly accord with the regular summer watering that container gardens tend to need; so the bulbs may not always prove very long-lived. But they are worth trying (and replacing if and when necessary) even if only for temporary effect.

For containers in sunny situations, choose *Crocus chrysanthus** varieties and other miniature crocus species (see Chapter 3), *Narcissus bulbocodium**, *Cyclamen coum**, *Iris histrioides* 'Major'*, *I. danfordiae**, *I. reticulata** and *Anemone blanda** to provide flowers in winter and spring.

*Oxalis adenophylla** is useful for early summer. And for late colour there are the autumn-flowering crocus*, of which the lilac-purple *Crocus medius* is a particularly easy and neat-growing choice. In a large container, the pink and white forms of *Cyclamen neapolitanum* (*C. hederifolium*)* will also provide an eye-catching autumn display; but the tubers of these can get rather big and leafy for the tiniest container mini-gardens.

The hardy cyclamen will grow happily in sun, if given plenty of peat in the planting mixture, but are also excellent for shady situations. Snowdrops and the yellow-flowered 'winter aconite', *Eranthis hyemalis*, are really too leafy and fast-spreading for small container gardens, although they are handy stand-bys for difficult shady positions. *E. cilicica* and *E.* × *tubergenii* 'Guinea Gold' are similar to the common winter aconite but less free-seeding and invasive, so better choices for very restricted planting spaces.

CHAPTER NINE

MINIATURE PLANTS UNDER GLASS

There are two main reasons for growing miniature plants under glass: to provide protection from winter wet for those high-alpines which are more than usually susceptible to rotting-off during damp weather at that time of year; and to house dainty winter-spring flowering plants and bulbs, for a particularly early display, unsullied by the ravages of the elements.

Specialist alpine nursery catalogues generally indicate quite clearly which plants are best given the winter protection of an alpine house or frame. They tend to be those with woolly or hairy foliage, some very tiny high-mountain cushion plants, and a few fleshy-leaved and rosette-forming plants, like the lewisias.

The advantage of having early-flowering plants and bulbs under glass is not only that they will bloom a little earlier and be that much lovelier when undamaged by the elements. The lack of weather damage also means that the display lasts much longer, and in a glasshouse it can be appreciated by the gardener in greater comfort and more leisurely than outdoors.

In addition, the protection that a glasshouse or frame affords against the worst of the winter freezes will help the gardener in growing some of those miniature plants which are not completely hardy; such as the more tender cyclamen species. And a glasshouse is also a wonderful place to grow highly fragrant plants, where their perfume may be appreciated to the full. Indeed, the delicate scents of many plants, which might go unremarked in the garden, become more powerful and noticeable under glass. This applies in particular to a number of miniature winter-flowering and spring-flowering bulbs; especially the crocus species and their varieties, many of which prove to be deliciously honey-scented under glass or when picked for the house.

□ The alpine house □

This is basically an unheated greenhouse with more-than-average ventilation built-in, since alpines do not need winter heat, and they hate being roasted in summer. Any greenhouse with plenty of panes which may be opened in hot weather is suitable.

Opposite: Saxifraga cochlearis *'Minor', one of the tiniest of the 'encrusted' saxifrages, ideal for the smallest of containers.*

Fig. 14   Rock plants in plunge beds
Pot-grown alpines, shrubs, conifers and bulbs under glass should be plunged to the rims of their pots in a bed of sand or grit, to conserve moisture and protect from extreme heat and cold.

A little thermostatically-controlled heat may be provided, solely to keep the temperature from dropping much below freezing during very cold snaps, especially if the plants include a few slightly tender types. However, any more heat than this bare minimum may well encourage loose, leafy growth which will spoil the compact-growing character of many alpine plants, shrubs and bulbs.

The plants are most commonly grown in pots and pans, plunged to their rims in beds and staging filled with sand or gravel (Fig. 14). One or two rocks may be set into the plunge material for effect, as recommended for rock gardens and raised beds outdoors. Tufa rocks planted with tiny alpines (see Chapter 8) are a particularly good choice under glass.

With this arrangement, you can ensure a constant but ever-changing display by bringing into the alpine house, from plunge frames, a succession of plants for different seasons.

Alternatively, beds (either raised or at ground-level) may be filled with a free-draining, gritty soil mixture, as advised for rock gardens, and be planted-up as permanent mini-gardens, complete with small rock outcrops and top-dressed with stone chippings.

□ Cold frames □

As already mentioned, these may be used for plunging pots of plants and bulbs waiting to go into the alpine house when their flowering season comes around. But it should be remembered that they can also be a feature in themselves where there is no glasshouse.

Here, again, plants and bulbs for winter and spring will provide an immaculate and extra-early display, while damp-hating plants will be protected from winter rains. And slightly tender plants will stand a better chance of surviving winter cold; especially if the glass is covered with sacking, newspapers or other insulating layers for added protection during prolonged and severe freezes.

The plants may be pot-grown, plunged to their rims in sand. Or the frame may cover a permanent mini-garden planted in a bed of well-drained soil mixture. Cold frames are both highly useful and very flexible.

□ Planting and maintenance □

The soil in permanently-planted ground-level beds should be prepared as for rock gardens (see Chapter 2). Fill raised staging beds for permanent planting with the mix recommended in the last chapter for container gardens; roughly equal proportions (by bulk) of soil-based potting compost, peat, and either grit or stone chippings.

This basic mixture will also do for the general run of rock plants, conifers, shrubs and bulbs in pots and pans. For plants which catalogues and reference books indicate as needing extremely gritty compost, the grit or chippings content may be increased to two parts (by bulk) to one part of soil-based potting compost and one part of peat. And where these trickier plants are to be grown in beds, be sure to work plenty of extra grit or chippings into the planting site.

Remember to top-dress beds and pots with stone chippings, to help keep the compost moist and the necks of low-growing plants dry, and to provide an attractive finish.

Lime-hating plants should be given the basic peat-bed mixture of roughly two parts 'ericaceous' peat potting compost to one part of coarse sand or lime-free grit. Do not top-dress with chippings (and certainly not with limestone chips).

Keep alpine houses and frames well ventilated whenever the weather is not freezing, and especially in summer. Provide temporary shading if plants start to suffer in hot spells.

Do not let the plants go short of water during spring and summer. But in autumn and winter, watering should be kept to the bare minimum required to stop the compost drying out completely. Always water carefully *around* the plants, rather than over their foliage; especially those with woolly or hairy leaves. Feed two or three times in spring and summer with a high-potash liquid fertilizer, to encourage free-flowering and sturdy growth.

Finally, watch out under glass for mouldy growths on leaves and stems, especially during damp autumn and winter weather. Aim to remove dead and mouldy leaves as quickly as possible, and treat affected plants with fungicide.

□ Plants for alpine house or frame □

Note: Where a plant name is followed by an asterisk * and little or no description is given, see Chapter 3 for further details.

The neat mat-forming kabschia saxifrages* are ideal choices for winter and early spring colour under glass, and their dainty button-flowers are especially lovely and long-lasting when protected from the weather.

Alpine primulas are also excellent, especially the *Primula marginata** varieties whose handsome toothed leaves retain their powdery silver-white coating best when sheltered from rain. Some, like the stunning *Primula allionii* (tiny sticky-leaved rosettes and large glistening flowers of white, pink or deep rose-red), must have glass protection against winter damp.

Many other neat-growing rock plants make superb alpine house or frame plants, including such gems as *Gentiana verna** and *G. acaulis**, the smaller encrusted saxifrages*, truly tiny alpine bell flowers like *Campanula raineri* and *C. zoysii*, the fleshy-leaved white, pink and apricot-flowered lewisias, and

Continued on p. 116

Primula *'Bileckii', one of the daintiest of the alpine primulas and a good choice for small container gardens.*

A well-stocked alpine house, with pot-grown rock plants, dwarf conifers and miniature shrubs plunged in a sand bed.

various high-alpine cushion and rosette plants such as the androsaces, dionysias and drabas which (like *Primula allionii*) must have winter rain protection.

Plants which enjoy cool, shady and moist conditions, such as *Ramonda myconi** and hardy cyclamen*, may be grown under alpine house staging, on the side of the alpine house away from the sun, or in shaded frames.

A number of cyclamen species are not quite hardy and make exquisite alpine house and frame plants. These include the fragrant pink or white spring-flowering *Cyclamen persicum* (the dainty wild parent of the popular houseplant cyclamen), *C. pseudibericum* (large scented rose-purple flowers in winter and early spring), *C. libanoticum* (large and very beautiful pale pink flowers, early spring) and *C. graecum* (handsome silver-marked leaves and pink autumn flowers).

The dwarf daphnes are wonderful little shrubs for growing under glass, their rich scent proving almost overpowering in an alpine house. And, of course, the tiniest dwarf conifers listed in the last chapter as suitable for container gardens are equally good, neat-growing choices for an alpine house or frame. Here, too, that minuscule and gnarled dwarf willow, *Salix × boydii**, will provide interest with its tiny silver-grey leaves.

And lastly, but by no means least, virtually all the miniature bulbs recommended in Chapter 3 for rock gardens and raised beds are suitable for alpine houses and frames. Remember that there are dwarf bulbs for summer and autumn flowers as well as for winter and spring.

Especially appealing and desirable are those which will provide a very early display under glass, while the rest of the garden is still deep in its winter sleep; such as *Cyclamen coum**, early-flowering crocus species*, and the enchanting dwarf irises, *Iris histrioides* 'Major'*, *I. danfordiae** and *I. reticulata**.

CHAPTER TEN

MINIATURE POOLS

A small pool adds the perfect finishing touch to such miniature-garden features as rock gardens, raised beds, planted paving, and small beds or borders packed with low-growing shrubs, plants and bulbs.

An ideal site is at the foot of a rock garden, where the lowest rockwork will provide a very handsome edging and background to the pool; especially if the rock crevices are planted-up with small ferns and other appropriate moisture-lovers. And at the base of a raised bed, a rock-outcrop border to the pool may again be contrived, to echo the rockwork on the bed above. Here, planting holes should be planned into the raised bed wall behind the pool site, so that ferns and trailing plants may overhang the water for a particularly luxuriant effect.

Planted paved and gravelled areas simply cry out for the addition of a little pool to complete the scene, especially if the area is intended for sitting-out in summer.

A small pool also looks very lovely and appropriate blending into a peat bed filled with moisture-loving and shade-loving plants; and the presence of the water-surface will help to create a moist micro-climate which peat-bed plants will greatly enjoy. A peat-block wall may divide the pool from the bed and be filled with small plants. Any overflow from the pool during heavy rain will serve to keep the peat blocks (and the planting mixture behind) nicely moist. Alternatively, a rockwork edging may be constructed to enhance both the bed and the pool, and to stop the peaty compost washing into the water during downpours.

The conifer-and-heather bed can also form an attractive partnership with a small pool. Here, again, a peat-block wall or rocks with low heathers spreading over the top will provide a handsome back-drop; and a poolside planting of small ferns will not look at all out of place in company with the heathers.

And, of course, a dinky little pool will add interest to any small border; but do take care in borders to site the pool well away from deciduous shrubs whose autumn leaves might clog the pool and cause problems. Contrive a little 'clearing' for it, towards the border-front and plant around with small perennials and low-growing evergreens.

Even in an ordinary garden border, rocks may be used to form a charming edging to the pool and a natural-looking break between soil and water. Indeed, rockwork and water go together so well that this combination should always be considered. But avoid simply plonking a line of small rocks all the way round

Above: *Rock plants and bulbs growing in a permanent bed, complete with rockwork, under glass.*

Opposite: *An attractive miniature pool edged with pebbles and moisture-loving plants, including a broad-leaved hosta and a yellow-flowered mimulus variety.*

the poolside. A single bold outcrop (such as you would construct for a rock garden) set behind and/or to one side of the pool will prove much more effective and natural in appearance.

□ Pool construction □

Cheapest of all is to use a plastic or PVC sheet to line the hole for your pool; but for preference choose long-lasting butyl rubber sheeting. Remember to line the hole with sand first, to cushion and protect the sheeting from sharp stones. Leave a decent-size overlap around the edges, and bury this beneath the soil or hide it under rocks, paving, pebbles, gravel etc.

Ready-formed rigid fibre-glass or plastic pools are simpler still. Make sure your hole fits the liner snugly and that the pool top is level, then disguise the edges as above.

The half-barrels sold by garden centres for planting will also make attractive

Fig. 15　Miniature pools

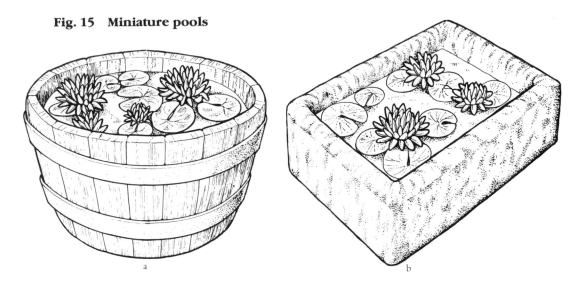

a　　　　　　　　　　　　　　　　　b

Tubs, deep troughs and other large planting containers may be turned into delightful miniature pools; either free-standing on a patio, or partially sunk into the ground. Make sure that any drainage holes or cracks are well sealed.

miniature pools (Fig. 15*a*) for paved or gravelled areas; either free-standing or partially sunk into the ground (which will give better protection from freezing in winter). Plug holes and cracks with a mastic sealant, or line with polythene. Deep concrete or reconstructed stone troughs and suchlike containers may also be utilized (Fig. 15*b*).

Remember that if the pool is to be planted with aquatics it should be about 60 cm (2 ft) deep. Any shallower, and it is likely to freeze solid during winter. In very cold regions, 75 cm (2½ ft) is advisable. And during prolonged hard freezes, an insulating covering is a wise precaution; especially for free-standing tubs or trough mini-pools on patios.

□ Miniature aquatic plants □

A small pool is only likely to offer enough growing space for one or two aquatic plants, and these should be miniatures suited to the size of the pool.

Your local garden centre is likely to offer a range of aquatics and poolside plants in spring, which is the best time to plant the pool. A wider variety can be found in the mail-order catalogues of specialist nurseries (see Useful Addresses).

Particularly suitable are the miniature varieties of waterlily, which will cover just a square foot or two of water surface per plant. Popular choices include *Nymphaea pygmaea* 'Alba' (starry white flowers), *N. p.* 'Rubra' (deep red), *N. p.* 'Helvola' (sulphur-yellow), *N. laydekeri* 'Lilacea' (carmine-pink) and *N. l.* 'Purpurata' (wine-red). Other neat-growing aquatics to look out for are: *Hydrocharis morsus-ranae* (the frog-bit; small waterlily-like leaf pads and white flowers), *Nymphoides peltata* (the water-fringe; again, miniature water lily-like leaves, and deep yellow flowers), *Hottonia palustris* (water violet; ferny foliage and lavender flowers; an elegant little oxygenating plant) and *Typha minima* (dwarf reedmace; brown bullrush-like heads).

APPENDIX: PLANT LISTS

These plant lists will help you to select small and miniature plants for different situations. They should prove particularly helpful, as an at-a-glance guide, when browsing through plant catalogues or visiting nurseries and garden centres.

▫ Key to plant lists ▫

Suitability for different garden situations is indicated as follows: RG/RB = rock garden or raised bed; W = wall garden; P = paving; B = border; PB = peat bed; CHB = conifer-and-heather bed; N = dwarf bulbs for naturalizing in grass; C = suitable for small container-gardens (e.g. troughs); G = good choices for growing under glass; S = shade tolerant; LH = lime-hater.

▫ Rock plants ▫

Obviously, all are suitable for rock gardens and raised beds. Some, however, are vigorous spreaders which may cause problems where planting space is very limited. these are marked 'V' in the following list.

Acaena microphylla P V
Aethionema 'Warley Rose'
Alyssum saxatile W V
Androsace G
Arabis W V
Armeria caespitosa P B C
   A. maritima B V
Aubrieta W P B V
Campanula carpatica P B
   C. cochleariifolia P
   C. garganica W
   C. × Laylodgensis
   C. portenschlagiana W P V
Cyananthus lobatus PB C S
Dianthus alpinus C
   D. deltoides W P B V
   D. 'La Bourbrille' C

   D. 'Whitehills' C
Dodecatheon B PB
Dryas octopetala P V
   D.o. 'Minor' P C
Gentiana acaulis P B C G
   G. septemfida B C
   G. sino-ornata (and other
      autumn gentians) PB C S LH
   G. verna C G
Geranium cinereum
   G. dalmaticum
   G. farreri (syn.
      G. napuligerum) C G
   G. sanguineum B V
   G. subcaulescens
Lewisia W PB C G S
Lithospermum LH

Mimulus cupreus 'Whitecroft Scarlet' B PB S
Nierembergia repens P
Oenothera missouriensis B V
Penstemon C
Phlox douglasii P B C
  P. subulata P B V
Polygonum vaccinifolium P B V
Primula allionii G
  P. auricula 'Blairside Yellow' C G
  P. 'Bileckii' C G
  P. marginata W C G
P. × pubescens C G
Pulsatilla vulgaris B
Ramonda W PB G
Saxifraga (Kabschia) C G
Saxifraga (encrusted) W C G
Saxifraga oppositifolia C
Sedum P B V
Sempervivum P B
Silene schafta W B V
Thymus P V
Viola cornuta P B
  V. labradorica 'Purpurea' P B S

□ Small perennial border plants □

Most are happy under ordinary border conditions, but some need or prefer the moist and lime-free soil of a peat bed.

Ajuga reptans S
Armeria maritima
Aster novi-belgii (dwarf Michaelmas daisies)
Astilbe (dwarf varieties) PB S
Campanula lactiflora 'Pouffe'
Dianthus (border pinks)
Dicentra eximia S
Dodecatheon PB S
Epimedium S
Euphorbia myrsinites
  E. epithymoides (syn. *E. polychroma*)
Fuchsia 'Tom Thumb'
Geranium endressii 'Wargrave Pink' S
  G. renardii
  G. 'Russell Prichard' S
  G. sanguineum
  G. wallichianum 'Buxton's Blue' S
Helleborus niger S
  H. orientalis S
Hosta (dwarf varieties) PB S
Incarvillea
Iris innominata hybrids PB S LH
  I. unguicularis (*I. stylosa*)
Meconopsis betonicifolia PB S LH
  M. cambrica S
Mimulus cupreus 'Whitecroft Scarlet' PB S
Oenothera missouriensis
Platycodon grandiflorum mariesii
Primula denticulata
  P. sikkimensis PB S
  P. × pruhoniciana 'Wanda' (syn. *P. juliana* 'Wanda') S
  P. vulgaris (wild primrose) S
Pulmonaria angustifolia S
Pulsatilla vulgaris
Roscoea cautleoides S
Sanguinaria canadensis 'Flore Pleno' PB S
Saxifraga (mossy) S
  S. umbrosa (London pride) S
Trillium PB S
Viola cornuta
  V. labradorica 'Purpurea' S
  V. odorata (sweet violet) S

□ Dwarf bulbs □

Anemone blanda RG/RB B N C
  A. nemorosa B PB N C S
Chionodoxa RG/RB B N
Crocus RG/RB B N C G
Cyclamen RG/RB B PB N C G S
Eranthis B N S
Erythronium B PB S
Fritillaria meleagris B PB N S

Rockwork and water always associate well, and the base of a rock garden is an excellent site for a small pool.

Galanthus B N S
Iris reticulata and similar species
   RG/RB B C G
Leucojum vernum B S
Narcissus asturiensis RG RB C G

N. bulbocodium RG/RB N C G
N. cyclamineus RG/RB PB N
   N. 'February Gold' (and
      other *cyclamineus*
      hybrids) B N

Oxalis adenophylla RG/RB B C
Rhodohypoxis RG/RB G
Scilla bifolia RG/RB B N
  S. sibirica RG/RB B N
  S. tubergeniana RG/RB B N
Sternbergia RG/RB B

Tulipa batalinii RG/RB G
  T. maximowczii RG/RB G
  T. tarda RG/RB B
  T. greigii varieties B
  T. kaufmanniana varieties B
  T. praestans varieties B

◻ Small and miniature shrubs ◻

Acer palmatum 'Dissectum'
  RG/RB B PB S
Andromeda polifolia PB C S LH
Berberis (dwarf varieties) RG/RB
  B
Betula nana RG/RB
Calluna vulgaris B PB CHB LH
Caryopteris × *clandonensis* B
Cassiope RG/RB PB LH
Ceratostigma B
Cistus B
Cytisus ardoini RG/RB C
  C. × *beanii* RG/RB B
  C. × *kewensis* RG/RB B
Daboecia PB CHB LH
Daphne cneorum RG/RB P C G
  D. retusa RG/RB C G
Erica herbacea (syn. *E. carnea*)
  RG/RB P B PB C
  E. cinerea RG/RB P B PB CHB
    C LH
  E. × *darleyensis* B PB CHB
  E. mediterranea P PB CHB

Fuchsia 'Mrs Popple' B
  F. 'Tom Thumb' B
Gaultheria PB S LH
Genista lydia B
Hebe RG/RB B
Helianthemuim RG/RB P B
Hypericum olympicum RG/RB P
  C
Magnolia stellata B
Pernettya B PB S LH
Philadelphus 'Manteau
  d'Hermine' B
  P. microphyllus B
Polygala chamaebuxus RG/RB
  PB LH
Potentilla PG/RB B
Rhododendron (dwarf varieties)
  RG/RB B B S LH
Rose (miniature varieties) B
Salix × *boydii* RG/RB C G
  S. lanata RG/RB B
S. reticulata RG/RB C
Vaccinium caespitosum PB S LH

◻ Dwarf conifers ◻

Abies balsamea 'Hudsonia'
  RG/RB C
Chamaecyparis lawsoniana
  'Ellwoodii' B CHB
  C. l. 'Ellwood's Gold' RG/RB
    B CHB
  C. l. 'Minima Aurea' RG/RB B
  C. l. 'Pygmaea Argentea'
    RG/RB B
  C. obtusa 'Nana' RG/RB C
  C. pisifera 'Boulevard' B CHB
  C. p. 'Plumosa Aurea Nana'
    RG/RB B CHB
Cryptomeria japonica
  'Vilmoriniana' RG/RB C
Juniperus communis

  'Compressa' RG/RB C G
  J. c. 'Depressa Aurea' B CHB
  J. procumbens 'Nana' B CHB
  J. squamata 'Blue Star' RG/RB
    B JCHB
Picea abies 'Nidiformis' RG/RB B
Picea glauca 'Albertiana Conica'
  RG/RB B CHB
  P. mariana 'Nana' RG/RB C G
Taxus baccata 'Standishii' RG/RB
  B CHB
Thuja occidentalis 'Rheingold'
  RG/RB B CHB
  T. o. 'Sunkist' RG/RB B CHB
  T. orientalis 'Aurea Nana'
    RG/RB B CHB

INDEX

ACKNOWLEDGEMENTS

The publishers are grateful to the author for granting permission to reproduce the colour photographs on pp. 87, 91, 94 and 114. The photographs on pp. 6 and 103 were taken by Jon Bouchier and are of the Alpine Garden Society Gold-medal award-winning display at the Chelsea Flower Show, 1989. All the remaining photographs were taken by Bob Challinor.

The publishers are also grateful to Michael Upward, Secretary of the Alpine Garden Society, for kindly suggesting suitable venues for the colour photographs, and to various garden owners for granting permission for their gardens to be photographed.

All the line drawings were drawn by Nils Solberg.